A-Z of
Key Concepts in
Primary Science

Malcolm Anderson

LearningMatters

First published in 2002 by Learning Matters Ltd.

British Library Cataloguing in Publication Data
A CIP record for this book is available from the British Library.

ISBN 1 903300 45 2

Cover design by Topics — The Creative Partnership
Text design by Code 5 Design Associates Ltd
Project management by Deer Park Productions
Typeset by PDQ Typesetting
Printed and Bound in Great Britain by Bell & Bain Ltd, Glasgow

Learning Matters Ltd
58 Wonford Road
Exeter EX2 4LQ
01392 215560
info@learningmatters.co.uk
www.learningmatters.co.uk

Contents

Introduction

Much has been said and written about the need to raise standards and how teachers should have high expectations of children in their classes. A key factor, among many, in raising standards is the quality of teaching that a child receives. An effective teacher will be inspirational, challenging, motivational and many, many other things. However, he or she will also be one who has a good grasp of the subjects they teach and the knowledge and understanding required in each one. Primary teachers are well known for their skill, enthusiasm and boundless energy and also for their wide range of professional expertise.

In recent years, great emphasis has been put on how important it is that teachers in all sectors develop sound and secure levels of subject knowledge. For without this sound and secure knowledge and understanding, it is very difficult for a teacher to meet the challenge of raising standards and developing high expectations. Good subject knowledge enables teachers to properly and adequately:

- plan and prepare appropriate schemes and activities for their children;
- ask questions that will extend and develop children's ideas and understanding of the world around them;
- identify children's alternative views and misconceptions;
- answer children's questions;
- impart knowledge about scientific concepts;
- develop skills of investigating through formulating questions and carrying out investigations.

It is vital therefore that teachers of primary science should have the skill, confidence and ability to help progress children's learning in science. Since the introduction of the National Curriculum, and later the DfEE/QCA Schemes of Work, there have been many resources made available to teachers to help them develop their understanding. But teachers are very busy people and, excellent though these resources are, a teacher sometimes needs to be able to dip into a resource just to check some details of a concept at fairly short notice, and because, sometimes, we cannot always remember everything!

The *A– Z of Key Concepts in Primary Science* has been written following a wish to be able to access key scientific knowledge and understanding in a quick, accessible, easy to read way. It is aimed at:

- classroom teachers who wish to confirm the background to concepts they are going to be teaching but don't have the time to read through the full chapter of a science textbook;
- trainee teachers as they continue to develop further their knowledge and understanding in order to gain Qualified Teacher Status.

The book is organised with straightforward alphabetical entries that are, when appropriate, cross-referenced to other items to help teachers make connections between key scientific concepts. A margin icon like this and bold type has been used to highlight cross-references.

Also included are suggestions of other printed, electronic and online resources that teachers might find useful when planning and teaching science lessons. Each resource is linked to a specific science topic. This icon appears when a resource is suggested.

The knowledge and understanding covered by the book addresses all the requirements of the National Curriculum at Key Stages 1 and 2, the areas of study in the DfEE/QCA Schemes of Work for Science and the requirement for Initial Teacher Training. By its very nature it cannot and does not attempt to cover everything — other texts do that very well. It is in essence an extended glossary. It is designed to be used as part of a teacher's toolkit, to confirm and develop your understanding and to give you confidence.

I hope you find this book of use and that it sits neatly not on your bookshelf... but on your desk!

Malcolm Anderson
June 2002

A–Z of Key Concepts

Acceleration

Acceleration is the rate of change or increase in the **velocity** of an object due to an increasing net force being exerted on that object. Velocity is the speed of an object in a particular direction so the rate of change in the velocity, or acceleration, refers either to a change in the speed or a change in the direction of the moving object. Therefore, if a car travelling in an easterly direction speeds up it is said to be accelerating. Likewise, if the car maintains its speed but goes round a corner it is also said to be accelerating. The opposite of this, an object slowing down, is called deceleration. Manufacturers often describe a car as being able to increase its speed from 0 to 50 m/s in 10 seconds. The acceleration of the car can be calculated as:

$$\text{Acceleration} = \frac{\text{Change of speed}}{\text{Time taken}} = \text{Change in speed per unit time}$$

The car's acceleration is therefore $\frac{(50 - 0)\text{m/s}}{10\text{ s}} = \frac{5\text{ m/s}}{\text{s}}$

Since acceleration is measured in metres per second per second, the speed of the car increases by 5 metres per second every second (5 m/s^2).

Newton's second law of motion is concerned with acceleration and states that when a force acts upon an object the object will start to move, speed up, slow down or change direction. The greater the force, the greater the change of movement.

Adaptation

In order to have survived and for the continuation of the **species**, animals and plants have adapted to the **environment** in which they have lived – their **habitats**. This adaptation includes responding to the **climate** and to the availability of food supplies and predators. In fact, adaptation can describe any of the features or characteristics of a living thing which help it to survive and can be described as being:

- functional – adaptations that have enabled survival in different **climates**;
- structural – adaptations that have allowed plants and animals to survive in different physical ways.

Air resistance

Air resistance is a frictional **force** that is exerted on objects as they travel through the air and causes them to slow down. It is a force that is described as working in the opposite direction to the forces that cause the movement of the object. It therefore opposes other forces. These forces include **gravity**.

We can see the effects of air resistance in everyday life and how, for example, it causes falling objects to slow down. If we drop a sheet of paper on the floor, or watch leaves falling from the trees in autumn, or a parachutist falling to Earth, we see air resistance in action. As the effects of the force of gravity pull the objects to the Earth, there is a counteracting force or upward thrust from the air. This opposing force causes the falling object to slow down, since one of the effects of a force is to make things slow down.

Changing the shape of the falling object in some way can change the effect of air resistance. Think again about the parachutist. As he or she freefalls from the aeroplane they are accelerating towards the ground until they reach a terminal velocity (the term used when forces acting on the object are balanced and it falls at a constant velocity) of about 10 m/s^2. When the parachute opens, their speed is suddenly and greatly reduced as the air fills the opening parachute. The surface area of the parachutist with their parachute has increased thereby increasing the effects of air resistance.

The same effect can be demonstrated using two identical pieces of paper, one open, one screwed up. The masses of the sheets of paper both remain the same but they will fall to the ground at different speeds. Because the flat piece has a greater upward thrust acting on it, it is subject to greater air resistance and will fall more slowly.

Amplitude

Amplitude is the height of a wave from the undisturbed or normal position to its crest. As the amount of energy within a wave is increased, then the amplitude also increases.

Although sound and light waves are different (sound waves are longitudinal waves and light waves are transverse waves), it is possible to illustrate how they react to increased energy levels. An increase in sound energy is indicated by the volume or loudness of that sound: the greater the level of sound energy that is put into a sound, the louder the sound will be. The same applies to light: the more energy there is in light, the greater the intensity or brightness of the light. Therefore, a sound wave that has high amplitude is a louder sound. Likewise, a light wave with high amplitude is a brighter light. We cannot 'see' the waves but by using measuring instruments (e.g. an oscilloscope), the amplitude of a sound wave can be shown on screen. The amplitude of a wave then is described as the extent to which the wave reaches from the normal.

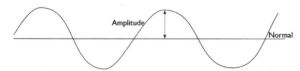

Amps

An amp or ampere is a measure of the flow of charge in an electrical circuit. This flow is known as an electrical **current**. The vibrating electrons transmit energy through the circuit. There is some flow of electrons but this is relatively slight compared to the flow of energy or charge. The higher the current within the circuit, the greater the flow of energy. The flow of the current, measured with an ammeter, is related to both the **voltage** and to the resistance within the circuit. Ohm's Law represents this relationship and states that the flow of charge, and therefore the amperes within a circuit, can be calculated as follows:

$$\text{Current (I)} = \frac{\text{Voltage (V)}}{\text{Resistance (R)}}$$

Animals

All **living things** (defined by their ability to carry out **life processes**) can be divided into one of five major groups or kingdoms. The animal kingdom is just one of these groups and consists of between 10 and 20 million species of living things. These are organisms that are multi-cellular and feed on plants, on other animals or on their remains. They are heterotrophic, which means they derive their nourishment from outside of themselves. Most animals, to some degree, can and do move about but there are some species that tend to spend most of their life in one place. The animal kingdom consists of a number of smaller groups or phyla. Some are **invertebrates** (animals without backbones) and some are **vertebrates** (animals with backbones).

The invertebrates are animals without a backbone and account for around 97% of animal species. Many invertebrates are soft bodied and live in water or damp places.

Kingdom: Animals		
Informal grouping: Invertebrate		
Phylum	**Characteristics**	**Examples**
Annelid worms	Annelid worms have segmented bodies, a round cross section and generally live in either soil, ponds or in sand.	Earthworms, leeches, lugworms and marine worms
Bryozoans	Bryozoans look like plants but actually consist of thousands of tiny animals.	
Cnidarians	Cnidarians have soft bodies and tentacles and live largely in marine habitats.	Corals, jellyfish and sea anemones
Echinoderms	Echinoderms have a skeleton of chalky plates with bumps, spines and pincers.	Starfish, sea urchins and sea lilies
Flatworms	Flatworms have non-segmented bodies and a flat cross section. Generally found in damp places such as ponds and inside other animals	Tapeworms and flukes
Molluscs	Molluscs have a soft body, often protected by a shell, and live on land, in freshwater and seawater.	Slugs, snails, clams, scallops, octopuses, squids and cuttlefish
Nematode worms	Nematode worms have non-segmented bodies and can be independent or parasitic living in soil and plants.	Roundworms
Sponges	Tube like animals found in marine habitats.	Sponges

The largest phylum within the informal classification of invertebrates is Arthropods. These are animals that have an exoskeleton, which is a hard case on the outside of the body. They also all share the characteristics of having segmented bodies and jointed legs.

Kingdom: Animals		
Informal grouping: Invertebrate Phylum: Anthropods		
Class	Characteristics	Examples
Arachnids	Nearly all arachnids live on land and most hunt for food. They all have eight jointed legs and some spin webs as a means of catching their prey.	Scorpions, spiders, mites, harvestmen
Chilopods	Chilopods have one pair of legs per segment of their body and hunt for their food.	Centipedes
Crustaceans	Most crustaceans live in a marine habitat although some do live on land but prefer damp conditions.	Water fleas, wood lice, crabs, lobsters, barnacles
Diplopods	Diplopods have two pairs of legs per segment of their body and eat decaying plants.	Millipedes
Insects	Insects have six jointed legs and a body divided into three sections: head, thorax and abdomen.	Dragonflies, butter-flies, grasshoppers, earwigs, stick insects, cockroaches

Those animals that are largely vertebrates belong to the phylum Chordates. Chordates are animals with a stiff chord that runs down their bodies, and of the 44000 species of Chordates almost all are vertebrates, although a few species have this stiff chord but are not regarded as being true vertebrates.

Kingdom: Animals		
Informal grouping: Vertebrate Phylum: Chordates		
Class	Characteristics	Examples
Amphibians	Amphibians have loose fitting damp skin, live in damp places and are cold-blooded or exothermic (i.e. obtain their heat from external sources, such as sunlight radiation).	Frogs, toads, newts and salamanders
Birds	Birds have skin covered with feathers, live in a wide vari-ety of habitats and are warm-blooded or endothermic (i.e. they generate their own heat within their bodies).	Ducks, geese, swans, eagles, hawks, finches and owls
Bony fish	As their name suggests, these fish have skeletons made of bone. They are exothermic, have a scaly skin and live in either freshwater or saltwater.	Eels, herrings, salmon, trout
Cartilagi-nous fish	Cartilaginous fish have skeletons that are made of carti-lage (gristle). Most are predators, have skin covered in scales, live in saltwater habitats and are exothermic.	Sharks, rays and skates
Jawless fish	Jawless fish do not have jaws or pairs of fins. Many filter their food from the water.	Lampreys and hagfish
Mammals	Mammals are endothermic, their skin is covered in hair or fur and they suckle their young. Most young develop inside their mother.	Opossums, koalas, kangaroos, duck billed platypus, bats, hedgehogs, ele-phants and humans
Reptiles	Reptiles are exothermic, have dry scaly skin and can live in dry, usually warm, conditions.	Snakes, lizards, tur-tles, crocodiles and alligators

Butterflies, Bugs & Other Beasties CD-ROM (Spiny Software) is an inter-active combination of references and games suitable for minibeast studies at Key Stage 2 and upper Key Stage 1.

Atmosphere

The Earth and all the living things on it are protected from the Sun by a huge 'blanket' or gaseous envelope called the atmosphere. This blanket, which is fairly uniform throughout its lower layers, consists largely of nitrogen (78%), oxygen (21%) and small amounts of other gases (about 1%), although this is dependent on altitude. It stretches about 1000 km up and is made up of a number of different layers:

- *Troposphere*. This layer stretches up 20 km from the Equator and 10 km at the Poles and is the only layer where living things can breathe nor-mally. It is also where the Earth's **weather** occurs.

- *Stratosphere*. This layer contains the gas ozone that absorbs harmful ultraviolet rays from the Sun. It can stretch up to 50 km above the ground but varies in thickness. Pollutants can cause thinning of the ozone layer, thus reducing its capacity to absorb harmful ultraviolet radiation. The temperatures in the stratosphere vary from about $-60°C$ at the bottom to just above $0°C$ at the top.

- *Mesosphere*. The top of the mesosphere is about 80 km above the ground and has temperatures as low as $-100°C$.

- *Thermosphere*. This is the hottest layer since there are very few air mo-lecules to absorb the radiation from the Sun. Temperatures at the top, 450 km from the Earth, can reach as high as $2000°C$. The thermosphere includes:
    - *the ionosphere*: contains many ions (atoms which have lost some electrons) and free electrons and is able to reflect radio waves;
    - *the exosphere*: here the air is very thin. Gas molecules exit from here into space giving this layer its name.

Atomic bonding

When atoms are joined together bonding takes place. All bonding involves the movement of electrons in the outermost shells of the **atoms**. Different atoms bond in one of three different ways. In salt, for example, the atoms transfer electrons from the outer layer of the sodium to the outer layer of the chlorine. This type of bonding is called **ionic bonding**. In compounds such as water, atoms share their electrons. This is called **covalent bonding**. In metals, the electrons flow around all the atoms, which is called **metallic bonding**.

Atoms

All matter is made up from tiny particles called atoms. An atom is the smallest part of an **element** and consists of **protons**, **neutrons** and **electrons**. Pro-tons, which are positively charged, and neutrons, which are neutral, join together at the centre of the atom to form the nucleus. Around the nucleus negatively charged particles called electrons orbit, a little like planets orbiting the Sun. These electrons are arranged in layers like the layers of an onion. These layers are called shells. More than 99.9% of an atom is empty space occupied by electrons.

In an atom of any particular element, there is always the same number of electrons and protons. It is the number of protons that gives the element its atomic number. So, for example, an atom of carbon has six protons in its nucleus, has six electrons surrounding it and has an atomic number of six. The element is also electrically neutral since the number of positively charged protons and negatively charged electrons are the same (the neutron is neutrally charged so does not affect the electrical charge of the atom). All the atoms of an element have the same number of protons. Some however have different numbers of neutrons. These are called isotopes. For example, carbon atoms usually have six protons and six neutrons in their nuclei with an atomic mass of 12. However, if the atom has eight neutrons, it would be an isotope. In this case, it would be called C–14, which is a radioactive isotope of carbon.

The atoms of different elements vary, with different masses and different colours. Atoms of one element can combine with atoms of another to form a new substance called a **compound**. Compounds are held together by **ionic bonding**, **covalent bonding** or **metallic bonding**. The larger particles in compounds are called **molecules**. For example, when two atoms of hydrogen (H) combine with one atom of oxygen (O) we get the compound **water** (H_2O). Atoms can also be brought together in a mixture where the atoms are not combined chemically but physically.

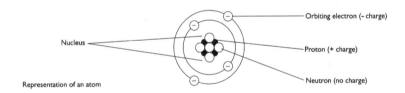

Nucleus

Orbiting electron (- charge)

Proton (+ charge)

Neutron (no charge)

Representation of an atom

Bacteria

Bacteria are single-celled microscopic organisms that can also live in colonies. The cells are much smaller than animal or plant cells and have no distinct cell nucleus. About hundred bacteria would fit onto a single printed dot.

Bacteria are all around us: some, like those that spread cholera and salmonella, are dangerous; others, like those used in the production of yoghurt and cheese, are useful. There are also millions of positive bacteria in the human body that assist in living processes such as digestion. Most bacteria get their energy from the breakdown of living or non-living organic matter.

Bacteria are active and play an important role in the **decay and decomposition** of plant and animal remains, and in returning nutrients to the soil, for example in the production of compost.

Balanced diets

Food is needed to help our bodies to move, to grow and to repair themselves after being damaged. While most foods are not unhealthy, many people eat unhealthy diets. The food that we eat and drink each day makes up our diet and it is important we eat a diet that contains a range of different foods since these different foods serve different purposes and provide us with different substances. A balanced or healthy diet is one that consists of the appropriate types of food in the correct quantities. There are seven nutritional categories:

1. *Proteins*: essential for the growth and repair of the body. Muscles, skin, hair and nails are nearly 100% protein. Bone is part protein.

2. *Fats and oils*: essential for the storage and release of energy, and as an insulator.

3. *Carbohydrates*: essential for the making, storage and release of energy and as roughage for the movement of food through the gut.

4. *Minerals*: essential for building bones and teeth, for the functioning of the nervous system and for the production of haemoglobin in red blood cells.

5. *Vitamins*: essential for the control of chemical reactions in the body and the control of deficiency diseases with symptoms such as poor vision, stomach pains, poor growth and weak bones.

6. *Fibre*: acts as roughage in the diet and prevents constipation.

7. *Water*: once broken down, the food we eat is dissolved in water in order to be absorbed by the body.

These are often combined into three groups that can be thought of as energy foods, body building foods and maintenance foods.

Food group	Foods	Functions
Energy: carbohydrates and fats	Bread, potatoes, pasta, rice, sugar, fatty and oily foods	Source of energy for movement and warmth
Body building: proteins	Meat, fish, dairy products, seeds, nuts	Growth and repair of the body
Maintenance: vitamins and minerals	Red meats, milk, fresh fruit, vegetables	Maintenance of healthy bones and teeth, prevention of 'vitamin deficiency' diseases

While we could survive without food for several weeks, we could only survive a few days without water. Most of the water we take in is through drinking, but most solid foods also contain water. Nevertheless, to maintain our bodily functions, we need to drink plenty of water every day, eat a diet that has a sufficient energy input level for our energy usage and ensure that there is a balance between the different food groups.

British Nutrition Foundation Posters (BNF) are two sets of A2 posters useful in supporting healthy eating in both Key Stages 1 and 2.

Balanced and unbalanced forces

When forces are balanced, no movement takes place (the forces are said to be equal and opposite). For example, in a tug of war contest, if each team is pulling with the same force then neither team will move forward, and the forces are therefore balanced. Once one of the teams exerts a greater force then they become unbalanced and the opposing team moves in the direction of the exerted force.

When forces are unbalanced, they are not equal to any opposing force and may be either greater or smaller. The net result is that when forces are unbalanced, movement takes place.

Batteries

The word battery is often misunderstood and misused. Strictly, a battery is two or more single-cell sources of **electricity**. For example, a 1.5 V unit is called a cell, whereas a 4.5 V unit is called a battery, i.e. three 1.5 V cells. However, not all cells have a voltage of 1.5 V.

A cell is the basic unit that produces electricity and has three main sections. There is a negative electrode, a positive electrode and a mixture of chemicals called the electrolyte.

A battery produces an electrical charge when chemical reactions in the cell cause electrons to flow out of the negative electrode, around the **circuit**, together with any devices in the circuit, and back via the positive electrode. As soon as the circuit is broken, the chemical reactions stop and the flow of electrons cease.

Batteries are convenient sources of electrical energy and have a variety of everyday uses.

Blood

Blood is the fluid in the body that carries oxygen to all the living cells within that body. It is like a transport system and, in addition to oxygen, it carries food substances, hormones and waste matter and helps the body to fight disease. Blood flows around the human body in a network of blood vessels (arteries, veins and capillaries) that total about 100000 km. The human body has about four litres of blood and a single drop contains millions of cells.

Most of these blood cells are red blood cells which contain a protein called haemoglobin, a pigment that gives the red blood cells their colour. The haemoglobin contains iron and is able to make temporary bonds with gas molecules. It combines with the oxygen when the red blood cells travel through the lungs and gives up the oxygen in exchange for carbon dioxide in other parts of the body. When it reaches the lungs again, it releases the carbon dioxide and collects more oxygen.

Blood also contains white blood cells which are larger than red blood cells although not as numerous. Their function is to surround foreign cells such as harmful bacteria and attack intruders such as viruses by releasing antibodies. White blood cells also contain platelets, which help the blood to clot. See **circulatory system** for details of how blood circulates in humans and other animals.

Body systems

The human body never ceases to cause wonder and amazement. It is a very complex and resilient organism that has a number of very significant and important systems within it. Each of these body systems has a specific function and consists of a number of structures or organs that together help perform that function. These functions are vital to the health and well-being of the body and are often interdependent on each other. The major systems of the human body are listed in the table below.

Name	Function
Circulatory	Carries food and oxygen to the body and also carries away carbon dioxide and other waste.
Digestive	Processes food from large food molecules into simpler substances that can dissolve in the bloodstream.
Endocrine	Regulates and controls specific body functions using hormones.
Excretory	Gets rid of waste and harmful substances from the body.
Immune	Helps the body to stay healthy by fighting germs.
Muscular	Causes voluntary and involuntary movement in the body.
Nervous	Controls and coordinates almost everything the body does.
Reproductive	Produces male and female sex cells for reproduction.
Respiratory	Ensures oxygen is made available to the body and waste is carried away.
Skeletal	Provides shape, support and protection to the body.

Further details of each body system are given individually.

Boiling point

When a liquid is heated, the particles gain more energy and move about more and more quickly. Those that are near the surface gain sufficient energy to escape (see also **evaporation**). As the **temperature** continues to rise, and more and more particles escape, the liquid molecules become gaseous and these bubbles of gas form inside the liquid as it reaches boiling point. These bubbles rise to the surface in a way that is characteristic of a boiling liquid.

The boiling point of different liquids varies and is an indication of how strongly the particles are held together in the liquid. Liquids with a low boiling point have weaker forces between their particles than liquids with a higher boiling point. Water boils at 100°C, but if salt is added, its boiling point is raised, so food cooking in boiling salted water will cook quicker than food in unsalted boiling water since it boils at more than 100°C.

Burning

When burning occurs, a number of irreversible reactions and changes take place. Most of these changes are chemical changes and are dependant on the presence of three things:

1. *Fuel.* These vary chemically in their nature but all contain sufficient levels of chemical potential energy. When burning occurs, they combine with the oxygen, and energy is transferred out from the fuel as both heat and light.

2. **Oxygen.** Oxygen combines with the carbon content of the fuel (most fossil fuels are mostly carbon and hydrogen) to produce carbon dioxide.

3. *Heat.* This is required to start the burning process. Most fuels have a temperature at which burning will begin, and heat is required to get the fuel to that temperature so that the burning reaction can begin. Once started, some of the heat energy from the burning fuel will be used to heat more fuel causing the reactions to continue.

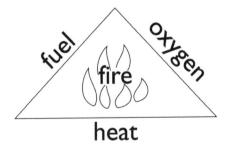

Cells

Every living thing is made up from cells. Each cell is essentially a simple building block in which the chemical reactions needed for life take place. Cells have the ability to repeatedly divide into two. Some living things are so small that they are made up from only one cell. The amoeba, for example, is a single cell organism. Other, much larger, living things such as humans have millions of cells. In fact, the human body contains about one hundred million, million cells, each one being about one hundredth of a millimetre in diameter. Although all cells share some basic characteristics, there is variation in shape and size since different cells perform different functions. In plants, some cells produce food during the process of **photosynthesis**; others are involved in growth or transporting food around the plant. In the human body, cells are often grouped together to form tissues (which in turn group together to make organs) or have a function within the blood or nervous system. Whatever their place each has a task to do.

Plant cells and animal cells are different but all living cells, whether plant or animal, contain three common features:

1. *Nucleus*. The nucleus of a cell contains structures called chromosomes that are composed of **DNA** (Deoxyribonucleic Acid) that can replicate itself to transmit genetic information from parents to offspring. It also controls all the reactions inside the cell.

2. *Cytoplasm*. The cytoplasm is a jelly-like substance where most of the chemical reactions in the cell take place. It contains organelles (mini-organs) such as mitochondria and ribsomes, each of which carry out different tasks.

3. *Cell membrane*. This forms the boundary of the cell. It is a very thin layer of protein that allows food and water to pass into the cell while allowing waste to pass out.

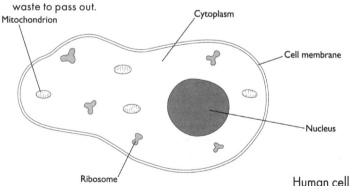

Human cell

Within the cells of a plant, there are three other features:

1. *Cell wall*. This is outside the cell membrane and holds the plant cell together. It is made of cellulose and is tougher than the cell membrane. Its main function is to support and protect the cell.

2. *Chloroplasts*. These are small bodies of chlorophyll which absorb light energy during the process of **photosynthesis**. They are only found in

13

green plant cells.

3. **Vacuole**. This is an area of watery liquid at the centre of the cell. It has two main functions: as storage space for food and to create pressure to keep the cell wall rigid.

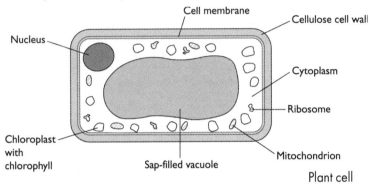

Plant cell

Chemical changes and reactions

When a chemical change or reaction occurs, new substances are formed as the molecular structure of the combined substances are broken down and recombined into the new substance. The bonds between particles, either atoms or molecules, of the substances concerned (either elements or compounds) are broken and, while some can be reversed, most chemical changes are irreversible.

Chemical changes can involve:

- *breakdown*: where the bonds become so unstable that they break— this is often caused by the application of heat;
- *combination*: where particles combine to make new substances;
- *rearrangement*: where particles break away and are then combined with other substances.

For example, when a cake is baked there is a chemical change. The baked cake looks and tastes different to the uncooked cake and the cooking cannot be reversed. A new substance has been formed. The new substance formed during a chemical change has not been created; rather it is the result of combining and changing other substances. The **mass** of the new substance therefore is equal to the total mass of the substances (reactants) involved in the chemical change or reaction. For example, the mass of the baked cake is equal to the mass of all the ingredients of the cake. Its volume may be different but its mass remains the same.

For a chemical reaction to take place the involvement of energy is required. When bonds are broken, there is a need for energy to be taken in, while making a bond actually releases energy. Endothermic reactions occur when heat is taken in in order for the chemical to bond to create new substances. Exothermic reactions are those where energy is released (e.g. when adding water to plaster of Paris).

Circuit diagrams

A circuit diagram is a way of drawing electrical circuits and identifying the components within that circuit using an agreed system of symbols.

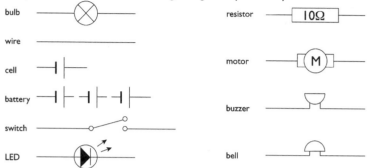

Circuits

A circuit is the route or path between two electrical terminals along which electricity can flow. This flow of electricity is called the **current**. There are two types of circuit, series and parallel.

A series circuit consists of just one route for the flow of electricity. If there is a break in the circuit, the electricity stops flowing. If you had a series circuit consisting of several bulbs and removed one then the circuit would be broken, the electricity would no longer flow and the other bulbs would not be lit. As you add more bulbs to a series circuit and thereby increase the resistance within the circuit, the intensity with which they burn is reduced as the voltage is shared out and the current becomes smaller. In any one series circuit, the current remains the same at any point within that circuit. Clearly, different circuits with different components will have different currents to each other.

Parallel circuits consist of several routes along which the electricity flows. If there were a break in a parallel circuit, the current would flow along an unbroken section. Bulbs in parallel circuits can be unscrewed without affecting the other bulbs in the circuit. As you add more bulbs to parallel circuits, the bulbs all continue to burn with the same intensity but the battery supplying the electricity would not last as long.

A short circuit occurs when an easier and shorter route is provided for the flow of electrons around the circuit. This often takes the current away from the components, causing them to stop working.

Circulatory system

The circulatory system is the major transport system within the human body and consists of **blood**, arteries, veins, capillaries and the heart. The system services all the organs of the body including the lungs, intestines, liver and kidneys as well as the rest of the human body.

In human circulation, as with all mammals and birds, there is a system of double circulation. Blood travels from the right side of the heart (right ventricle) to the lungs. Here it exchanges carbon dioxide for oxygen and becomes bright red, before returning to the left side of the heart (left atrium). The second loop in the system involves the blood now being pumped from the left ventricle around the body. Here, it loses the oxygen it has carried and gains carbon dioxide before returning to the right atrium of the heart, for the process to begin again.

The heart is a large muscle that is effectively a pump. It pumps blood around the body through a series of blood vessels. There is 100 000 km of blood vessels in the human body. Some of these vessels are arteries and carry oxygenated blood away from the heart. Arteries have strong thick walls that allow the blood to travel at high pressure and are generally deep within the body, except in the wrist and neck. Here, the pumping action can be felt as blood passes pulse points. Veins that carry deoxygenated blood back to the heart, have thinner walls. They also include valves to prevent the deoxygenated blood from flowing in the wrong direction. The arteries and veins are linked by a network of very small capillaries that have walls so thin that they allow substances like oxygen and hormones to pass out of the blood into cells. These capillaries occur throughout the body and are so small that they can only be seen using a microscope.

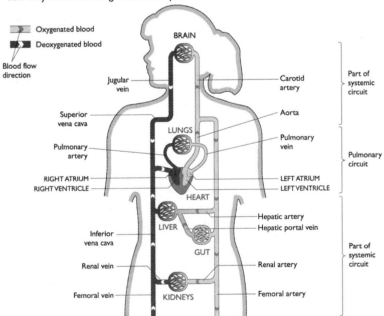

Other animals have different circulatory systems. A fish, for example, has a heart with two chambers and its blood flows in just a single loop. The blood travels through the gills (where it collects oxygen) then around the body delivering oxygen and collecting carbon dioxide. It then returns to the gills with the carbon dioxide. A frog's heart, however, has three chambers. Blood flows in two loops, one through the lungs to gain oxygen, the other around the body to give up the oxygen.

Classification

At its very simplest level, classification allows us to split every thing into two groups: 'living things' and 'non-living things' (although some may include 'never lived' as a third category). The world of living things uses a system of classification to help sort and identify the millions of different organisms of varying complexity and size that there are in the world. At the primary level, it is sufficient to divide living things into two groups, plants and animals, but the full classification system now identifies five major groups or kingdoms. The full classification system is:

Kingdom	The largest grouping in classifying living things.
Phylum	The name given to a major group within a kingdom, sometimes called a division.
Class	A class is a major group with a phylum.
Order	An order is a part of a class; some classes are split into many orders.
Family	A large collection of species that have things in common.
Genus	A smaller collection of species that have features in common.
Species	A group of living things that can breed naturally together.

The five kingdoms of living things are:

Animalia	The animal kingdom contains organisms that feed on plants or other animals. There are between 10 and 20 million species.
Plantae	The plant kingdom contains some 400 000 species of organisms that produce their own food using sunlight.
Fungi	Fungi absorb food made by plants and animals and include mushrooms, toadstools and yeast. There are over 100 000 species.
Monera	This kingdom includes bacteria, the simplest form of life on Earth. There are some 4000 species.
Protoctista	This kingdom contains over 65 000 species of simple organisms that mostly have a single cell. Most Protoctista live in water.

Climate

Climate is often regarded as the weather in a place averaged out over a long period of time (three months or so). The climate of an area or region depends on its position on the Earth's surface. For example, land near the Equator has a hot climate because it gets sunshine from almost directly overhead. As you travel further away from the Equator, the climate is cooler until you reach the North and South Poles where the Sun is always low on the horizon and the temperatures are constantly low.

There are, however, other factors that affect climate. For example, the oceans carry warmth around the world and affect the land climate, as do winds and the height of land above sea level.

Climates are classified into eight main groups, within which there are also variations.

Climate	Characteristics
Polar	Very cold and dry strong winds
Tundra	Cold with low rainfall and short summers
Mountain	Climates depend on latitude and altitude
Cool temperate	Not very hot summers or very cold winters
Warm temperate	Mild wet winters, hot dry summers
Desert	Very hot days and very cold nights, very little rain
Monsoon	Sudden changes from dry to wet weather
Tropical	Very hot with heavy rainfall

The climate of a region affects the **plants** and **animals** that live there. Different plants and animals are most suited, and have adapted well, to particular climates, and so thrive there. For example, bears are well suited to living in the cold polar regions because of the food they eat and the thickness and the type of their fur. On the other hand, an elephant would not survive in such conditions due to its diet of vegetation, the speed at which it moves and its unprotected skin.

There are a number of climatic factors that affect **living things** and their **environment**, including temperature, light intensity, rainfall and wind speed. The most profound of these climatic factors is without doubt **temperature**. Generally living things prefer to live in an environment with warm temperatures and a supply of water and food. This is why, as you travel from temperate climates to ones that are more extreme, like the poles or deserts, there is a marked reduction in the number of species of living things to be found.

Colour

Our world is a very colourful place (without colour, we would not be able to learn as much about our surroundings as the colours of nature often act as a warning of danger). We are able to see colours because our eyes can distinguish the different wavelengths of visible light from the **electromagnetic spectrum** as different colours. The longest wavelength that we are able to see is red, while the shortest is violet. The other colours of the spectrum lie between these two. The full spectrum is:

- Red
- Orange
- Yellow
- Green
- Blue
- Indigo
- Violet

The mnemonic, 'Richard Of York Gained Battle In Vain', is just one of many used to help remember the correct order of the spectrum.

These colours are all contained in white light. When white light is passed through a prism it is split into the seven constituent colours. This is called diffraction and is caused by the different colours of light travelling at different speeds in the prism. Exactly the same process occurs in droplets of rain, creating a rainbow.

Of the seven colours, three – red, green and blue – are primary colours and can be combined to create all the other colours in the spectrum, and indeed almost any other colour. Where two primary colours overlap, they produce secondary colours.

Primary colours	overlap to make	Secondary colours
Red and blue		Magenta
Red and green		Yellow
Green and blue		Cyan
Red, green and blue		White

The nerve cells in our eyes are only able to detect these three primary colours, so we see other colours because of the very many combinations and proportions used. We see the colours of objects because when light is reflected from an object into our eyes, the only colours to be reflected are those that match the pigment in the colour of the object. The rest is absorbed.

For example, if you look at a red object under white light, only the red light is reflected (the other colours are absorbed). Similarly, if you look at a red object under a red light, the object would still appear red since only the red light is reflected anyway. If, however, you were to look at a red object under a blue light (through a filter which only allowed blue light to pass through and blocked red and green), then the object would appear black since the pigment in the object would absorb the blue light and there is no red to be reflected.

So shining different coloured lights on objects can cause them to seemingly take on a different colour. A cyan object, for example, looks black in red lighting but green in yellow lighting. To work out what colour different coloured objects will appear, start with the primary colours in the light, take away the colours that the object absorbs and you are left with the reflected colours. (Note that it is very difficult to obtain good, effective colour filters in primary schools and virtually impossible to set up conditions to mix coloured lights to obtain satisfactory secondary light colours or white light.)

The primary colours of light and the primary colours of paint and pigments are different. Whereas the colour mixing of light involves adding colours, colour mixing in paint involves subtracting colours. Pigments absorb different colours of light (i.e. blue light absorbs all colours except the blue range, red absorbs all but the red range, etc.). If pigments were 'pure', mixing all of them would produce black, as all colours would be absorbed. In reality, paint pigments are mixtures and rarely absorb all the wavelengths. Thus mixed paints always reflect some traces of colour so, when mixing them together, we are more likely to see a muddy brown. The primary colours of pigment are related to the secondary colours of light but we usually refer to them as yellow, blue and red.

If the proportions of pigment and light are varied, then the number of possible colours produced is huge. Even though we may sometimes find it difficult to distinguish different colours, our eyes are actually capable of distinguishing more than 20 000 shades.

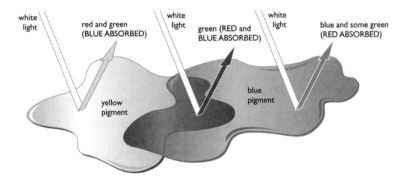

The 100 Science Lessons series (Scholastic) provides useful ideas for children in Key Stage 2 learning about colour.

Compounds

A compound is a substance consisting of definite proportions of atoms of two or more **elements** that bond together in a chemical reaction. Once this reaction has taken place, it is very difficult to separate the different elements. Compounds are held together by either **ionic bonding** or **covalent bonding**. Water is a good example of a compound in that it is made up from two atoms of hydrogen together with one atom of oxygen. Compounds are different from elements, in that in a compound a chemical reaction has taken place. In a mixture of elements, the elements are simply mixed together, such as oxygen and nitrogen in the atmosphere. It is also possible to have mixtures of compounds that do not react together, such as a mixture of dry salt and flour, or dry sand and iron filings.

Compression

Compression is a pressing together or bunching up. Materials can be compressed into a smaller space. Gases are more easily compressed than solids and liquids. Waves can also be compressed. When sound travels through the air, the vibrating sound causes alternate compressions and decompressions in the air molecules.

Condensation

Condensation occurs when water vapour in the air comes into contact with a cooler surface and changes from a gas into a liquid as its temperature falls. The cold surface removes heat energy from the water vapour so turning it into a liquid.

Condensation can be observed as a weather phenomenon in two ways:

1. *Mist or fog.* When humid air near the ground is cooled by cool air sinking towards the ground, the result is mist or fog.

2. *Dew.* When humid air comes into contact with a cold surface such as the ground, or objects near ground level, the humid air cools and condensation can be seen on the ground as dew. If the temperature is above $0°C$, then the condensation will be in the form of dew. If it is below $0°C$, then the condensation will freeze and will be seen as frost.

Conductors – electrical

An electrical conductor is a material or body that will allow an electric current to flow through it easily. The electric current is simply the flow of electrons around a circuit.

Metal is a very good conductor of electricity because all metals have **free electrons**. This means that the electrons are not attached to an atom, molecule or ion, but are free to move under the influence of an electric field. Because of this, metals are used for wires, fuses and electrical cables. Some liquids are also conductors of electricity, such as liquid metals like mercury and molten iron. Sodium chloride solution (salt water) will also conduct electricity.

Materials that do not conduct electricity are called **insulators**. (Note that if there is enough electricity present, for example lightning, electricity will travel through anything!)

Conductors – thermal

A thermal conductor is one that will permit heat to flow through it by conduction. This means that when one part of a substance is heated, its molecules vibrate more violently. This has a knock-on effect on neighbouring molecules and so the heat energy is passed on. This transfer of energy takes place because materials which are good conductors, such as metals, have a number of **free electrons** that move around absorbing heat from the heat source.

Different materials conduct heat by different amounts. While metals make good thermal conductors, gases are very poor conductors (the atoms are further apart) and while water will conduct some heat, it is generally a poor conductor.

Conservation of energy

Energy comes in many different forms — for example, heat, light and sound. We often can, and do, change energy from one form to another. When you turn on a light, electrical energy changes to light energy and heat energy. When this change or conversion takes place, there is some waste heat produced but no energy is lost. It has simply changed, even though some may have left the system. Energy therefore can neither be created nor destroyed, simply changed from one form to another, hence it is conserved.

Conservation of mass

The law of the conservation of mass states that, in a system, mass or matter can neither be created nor destroyed. It can, however, undergo either a **physical** or **chemical change**. When a change in the state of a matter occurs, the physical properties of the matter will change. Its mass, however, remains constant. If 100 g of ice were melted, you would have 100 g of water. This could be boiled to make 100 g of steam, although this is difficult to measure. If all the steam could be collected and condensed, it would again form 100 g of water. Freezing would again produce 100 g of ice. Similarly, a candle with a mass of 100 g, which is burning may appear to burn away to nothing, but it actually produces 100 g of products. This is called the conservation of mass.

When chemical changes occur, new substances are often formed which makes it difficult to reverse the changes. The total amount of material, however, will remain the same. Even though matter may have changed appearance, it cannot be destroyed nor created — it is simply changed into something else.

Consumers

Animals are unable make their own food so feed on plants or other animals in a **food chain**. They are therefore consumers. They often eat more than one kind of food so become part of more than one food chain. Some eat only plants and are called herbivores; others eat only animals and are called carnivores. Those that eat both plants and animals are called omnivores. Primary consumers are those that eat only plants (producers), secondary consumers eat primary consumers, tertiary consumers eat secondary consumers and so on.

The food any particular consumer eats may fluctuate in its availability due to a variety of reasons such as:

- disease;
- competition for resources;
- climatic changes;
- human activity.

If any of these occur, then the consumers may respond and may need to:

- seek other food;
- move to an area where the food is in greater supply;
- adapt to climatic change over time.

Failure to respond to availability of food, and the result of disease, may lead to the death of that organism with the consequences being felt by other consumers.

Covalent bonding

In covalent bonds, the electrons are shared between the atoms in pairs called electron pairs. The smallest part of a **compound** with covalent bonds is a molecule. The bond between the atoms within each molecule is strong, but the forces that attract the molecules are weak, and consequently many covalent compounds are **liquids** or **gases**. Their low boiling and melting points occur because the bonds between the molecules are easily broken.

Current

Electricity is a form of energy and has many uses since it can be changed into other forms of energy such as heat, light and sound. It is also easy to use because it can flow along wires to where it is needed. This flow, which is called an electric current, is a flow of electrical charge and is measured in **amps** or amperes. A current of one amp amounts to about 6 000 000 000 electrons passing any one point in a second.

Electrical currents in **circuits** behave a little like water being pumped around a system of pipes. The electrons are moved around the circuit because a 'push' is given to them by an energy source such as a battery. The electrons cannot leave the circuit and are all moved at the same time with no bunching or spreading out and, contrary to popular belief, they actually flow from the negative end of the battery to the positive. This occurs because the electrons have a negative charge and are attracted to the positive terminal of the battery, like unlike poles of two magnets.

Electricity is an electromagnetic process. If a circuit is broken, then the current stops flowing, but, unlike a break in a water pipe, none of the electrons will escape. Similarly the electrons in a circuit cannot be used up: if there is a break in the current flow, it may be due to the energy source (a battery) being converted to heat or light.

The current in a circuit can be increased by, for example, increasing the power source by using a higher voltage battery, akin in the water system to turning up the pump to push the water faster. Thus an increased voltage would increase the current (rate of flow) in a circuit.

However, there is another factor that affects the current. If the flow of charge in a circuit meet a material that slows down its flow, it is said to have met some **resistance**. In the water system example, this would be like the flowing water meeting a smaller bore of pipe that causes a resistance to the flow of the water. In an electrical circuit, this could be a component such as a lamp or a buzzer.

In series circuits (see **circuits**), where all the components are connected end to end, there is only one possible route for the current to flow. This means that the resistance offered is the same for all electrons and the current therefore remains the same. But in parallel circuits (see **circuits**), where components may be connected side by side and some of which may have a different resistance to others, then the flow of the electrons may vary in different parts of the circuit.

$$\text{Current (I)} = \frac{\text{Voltage (V)}}{\text{Resistance (R)}}$$

Day and night

Day and night occur as the Earth rotates about its axis causing one half of the Earth to always be facing the Sun while the other half is in darkness. If you were to look down on the Earth high above the North Pole, you would see that the Earth's rotation is in an anticlockwise direction. It is the Earth's rotation that accounts for day and night and it is the direction of movement that explains why the Sun 'rises' in the east and 'sets' in the west. In reality, the Sun does not rise, since its position is fixed. It is the Earth's movement that causes the apparent movement of the Sun across the sky.

The length of daylight varies throughout the year. This is due to the inclination of the Earth's axis. The Earth does not rotate about a vertical axis but is tilted at an angle of 23.5° and always points towards the star Polaris. The variations caused by this inclination also account for the seasons (see **seasons**) and mean that, in Britain, the greatest length of daylight hours in midsummer can be as much as 18 hours, whereas the shortest in midwinter can be as little as six hours.

These hours vary depending on latitude. For example, the further north from the Equator you travel in summer (when the northern hemisphere is tilted towards the Sun), the longer the daylight hours, so there are times at the North Pole when the Sun does not 'set'. Likewise in winter (when the northern hemisphere is tilted away from the Sun), there are times at the North Pole when the Sun never 'rises'.

Decay and decomposition

When living things, both plants and animals, die, the process of decomposition begins. This means that they are broken down, often very quickly, into much simpler substances and dispersed into the environment by other living things that use the decaying organism as a source of food. These other living things are known as decomposers and produce enzymes (proteins which act as catalysts in chemical reactions) that digest the dead material and provide food for the decomposer. This process is called decay. When an animal dies, other living things such as maggots (the larvae of flies) act as decomposers and begin to feed on the decomposing body.

When the decomposing material has been broken down sufficiently much smaller organisms, such as bacteria and fungi, begin to work it. The whole decomposition process therefore is also part of **food chains and webs**, in that these decomposing plants and animals provide food for other living things, which in turn will be a source of food for something else.

Density

The density of a material is described as its mass per unit volume. The **mass** is usually measure in kilograms (kg) and volume in cubic metres (m^3), so density is measured in kg per m^3. To illustrate this, think about the materials, lead and balsa wood. If the pieces were identical in weight (see **mass and weight**), their volumes would be very different since the density of the lead, at 11 340 kg per m^3, would be much greater than that of the balsa wood at 198 kg per m^3.

The density of a particular material relative to the density of water, fresh or salty, affects its ability to float. If the overall density is less dense than water, the object will float (see **floating and sinking**). Thus balsa wood floats and lead sinks.

Digestive system

The digestive system is responsible for the breaking down of food into small particles and the absorption of various substances into the body for transportation around the body in the **circulatory system**. This process consists of physical processes and chemical processes.

The physical processes consist of chewing the food in the mouth, using **teeth** to cut up and grind down the food into smaller pieces before it is swallowed. This increases the surface area of the food allowing enzymes (proteins produced by living cells which act as catalysts) to act more quickly. Muscles in the gullet aid this process and, as they contract, they push the food towards the stomach. Here, the physical process continues as muscles in the stomach wall contract and churn the food to allow for better digestion through the chemical process. The chemical process breaks down the chemicals in the food (through chemical reactions) into smaller molecules that become soluble and also small enough to be absorbed through the wall of the gut into the body. This chemical process uses different enzymes that speed up these chemical reactions.

The first enzyme, amylase, is actually introduced during the chewing process and breaks down starch. Other enzymes are added at different stages of digestion. In the stomach, the gastric gland produces gastric juices that contain the enzyme pepsin that breaks down proteins. These glands also produce hydrochloric acid that again helps to break down protein and also kills germs in the stomach. As the food reaches the pancreas, more enzymes are released causing the breakdown of starch to sugars, proteins to peptides and fats to fatty acids and glycerol. In the duodenum, the liver produces a liquid called bile which breaks up fat into small droplets that can then mix with other liquids. More enzymes break down substances in the ileum, and it is also here that small molecules of digested food are absorbed into the bloodstream.

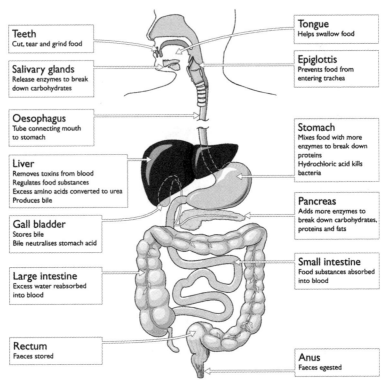

Teeth
Cut, tear and grind food

Salivary glands
Release enzymes to break
down carbohydrates

Oesophagus
Tube connecting mouth
to stomach

Liver
Removes toxins from blood
Regulates food substances
Excess amino acids converted to urea
Produces bile

Gall bladder
Stores bile
Bile neutralises stomach acid

Large intestine
Excess water reabsorbed
into blood

Rectum
Faeces stored

Tongue
Helps swallow food

Epiglottis
Prevents food from
entering trachea

Stomach
Mixes food with more
enzymes to break down
proteins
Hydrochloric acid kills
bacteria

Pancreas
Adds more enzymes to
break down carbohydrates,
proteins and fats

Small intestine
Food substances absorbed
into blood

Anus
Faeces egested

By the time the colon is reached, all the digestible food has been broken
down and absorbed into the body. What is left is indigestible foods such as
roughage and water. In the colon, water is also absorbed into the blood
leaving behind semi–solid waste. This waste collects in the rectum before
being passed out of the body, through the anus, as faeces.

Dissolving

The process of dissolving occurs when **materials** are broken down into
molecules. The gaps between the molecules of one material are then filled
by the molecules of the other material. Solute particles are sometimes bigger
than the particles of the solvent (e.g. sugar particles in water). We generally
think of dissolving as a process that occurs in a liquid such as water and,
although this is not always the case, it does provide us with a good example.

Dissolving requires the presence of a solute and a solvent. The solute is the
material that is going to be dissolved and the solvent is the material that it will
dissolve in. A substance that will dissolve is said to be soluble, and one that
will not is said to be insoluble. Salt and sugar are examples of solutes while
water is a solvent. When solutes are placed in a solvent, the solute is broken
down into molecules as the solvent breaks the bonds between the particles of
the solute. These particles are now so small that they cannot be seen between
the tiny particles of the solvent and fit themselves into the gaps between the
particles of the solvent. The resulting material is called a **solution**.

Different solvents can be used to dissolve different solutes and to produce different solutions. They do not always need to be in a combination of solids and liquids: for example, gases can also dissolve in water. Fizzy drinks contain a gas (carbon dioxide) that is forced to dissolve in the water in order to fit into the bottle. Likewise, it is possible to dissolve solids together.

The speed at which materials will dissolve can vary depending on a number of factors:

- *Size*. Large granules of a solute dissolve more slowly than smaller particles because the solvent acts on the surface area of the solute. In cooking, fine table salt dissolves much quicker than sea salt.

- *Temperature*. A warm solvent contains more energy than a cold solvent (the molecules are therefore moving more slowly). This means that in a warm solvent the granules will be broken down much more quickly. When you have a drink, sugar dissolves more quickly in a hot drink than in a cool drink.

- *Agitation*. If the solute and solvent are agitated by stirring, the speed of dissolving increases. Again, this is due to an increased energy level. When you add sugar to a hot drink, stirring aids the dissolving process. If it is not stirred, some of the sugar often remains at the bottom of the cup.

Just as solutions can be made, so too can they be separated. See **solutions**.

Diversity of organisms

It is thought that the number of species of organisms living on the Earth is between 12 and 100 million. Of that number, only about 1.4 million have been identified. The rest are either yet to be discovered or identified, or there is some disagreement as to how they should be classified. All of these known species have been grouped using the system of **classification** in a hierarchical system. This reflects the very rich diversity of organisms and allows us to begin to study and understand more about them.

DNA

DNA – or deoxyribonucleic acid – is a **molecule** that is found in the cells of living things and carries coded instructions that are passed on to future generations. This genetic information determines how the plant or animal will grow and develop. It carries the 'blueprint' or instructions for the functions of each cell, these instructions being divided into units of information called **genes**. Most genes are coded instructions for making particular proteins. When a particular protein is required, the part of the DNA code for that protein is copied. DNA can replicate itself to carry genetic information from a parent to their offspring.

Earth

The Earth is the only planet in the **Solar System** that has an **atmosphere** containing appreciable amounts of oxygen to support life. It also has a surface with rivers, lakes and oceans and the ability to support a huge range of **living things** such as **plants** and **animals.** Some 5000 million years ago the Earth did not exist, it was simply a spinning cloud of gas and dust. Over millions of years, the gas clumped together, cooled and formed a planet. The atmosphere formed and, over time, plants and animals evolved. It is thought that the Earth has a dense core of molten iron, with a temperature of 4000°C, a less dense mantle with temperatures between 1500 and 4000°C and then a crust that is about 50 km thick. The Earth spins on its own axis once every day, orbits the Sun once a year and has a satellite in orbit around it called the **Moon**.

Eclipses

There are two types of eclipse, solar and lunar, both of which can be either partial or total in their coverage and effect. A solar eclipse occurs when the Sun, Moon and Earth align themselves. The Moon causes a shadow to be cast on certain parts of the Earth. A total solar eclipse occurs when the Moon passes completely in front of the Sun masking the Sun entirely. A lunar eclipse occurs when the Sun, Earth and Moon are aligned in that order. Again a shadow is cast. This time the Earth casts a shadow on the surface of the Moon. Lunar eclipses can only ever be observed at night and occur when there is a full moon.

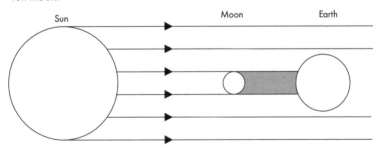

A Solar Eclipse (not to scale)

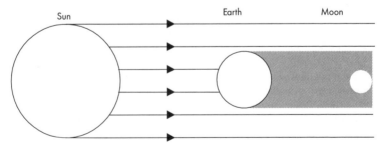

A Lunar Eclipse (not to scale)

Ecosystems

An ecosystem is a very distinct area that contains not only the many plants and animals that may be living on, over or under the area but the actual physical environment, the rocks, the soil and the air above. Ecosystems are distributed all over the Earth and are mainly grouped by **climate**, ranging from tropical rain forests and deserts to polar ice caps and tundra. From the cold and dry regions around the Poles to the hot and wet regions around the Equator, each ecosystem has living within it plants and animals that have adapted to the particular conditions of the area.

Within these **habitats,** plants and animals have formed interdependent communities, each having a particular role as they compete for food and resources in order to survive. Together these plants and animals form **food chains and webs**. These habitats provide most of the food that its inhabitants require and can vary greatly in size.

Characteristics of Ecosystems		
Ecosystem	Main characteristics	Locations
Polar regions	Very low temperatures	Arctic (North Pole) Antarctic (South Pole)
Seashores	Half land, half sea Constantly changing	Around the edges of all continents and land masses
Towns and cities	Varied temperatures depending on location More sheltered than countryside Built-up habitats for humans	All around the world
Mountains	Varied climatic conditions according to height	All continents
Rivers and lakes	Freshwater ecosystems supporting a wide range of plant an animal life	All around the world
Grasslands	Largely grass with only some other plants and animals	Mainly Asia, North and South America and Africa
Oceans	The largest ecosystem of all taking up two-thirds of the Earth's surface	All around the world
Rainforests	Very hot and wet with large numbers of species of plants and animals living there	Central and South America, central Africa, Southeast Asia and northern Australia
Wetlands	Both freshwater and saltwater marshes and bogs	All continents except Antarctica
Deserts	Mostly very hot, cold at night with hardly any rain	North and South America, Asia, Africa, Australia
Woodlands	Usually found in temperate climates Contain conifer and broad-leaved trees	Many parts of the world

Elasticity

Elasticity is the property of a material that allows it to return to its original shape and size when forces acting upon it have been removed. Rubber, for example, has the property of elasticity. When it is pulled it stretches; when the force is removed it shrinks back to its original size.

However, if the force exerted on the material is sufficiently large, then it is possible to break the molecular structure of the material and for the shape and size to be altered. At this point, it is said to have reached its elastic limit.

Many organic compounds are elastic, both natural (like skin) and synthetic (such as plastics).

Electrical components

Electrical components are devices that are connected into an electrical circuit (see **circuits, circuit diagrams**) and perform a specific function. Electrical components can be vast complicated pieces of machinery or tiny devices such as lamps and buzzers. Devices work because the current flowing around a circuit meets fixed atoms in the circuit causing them to vibrate more. In a lamp, this causes the filament (a high resistance material) of the lamp to become hot and emit a light.

There is an internationally accepted set of standard symbols for denoting the various components in electrical circuits when drawing **circuit diagrams**.

Electricity

Electricity is an accepted and essential part of everyday modern life for millions of people throughout the world. It is something we take for granted and can be used on demand at the flick of a switch. Electricity has become increasingly useful because:

- it is a form of energy that can be easily and conveniently moved from one place to another;
- it is easily converted into other forms of energy such as heat, light and sound;
- it can be quite easily generated from fuel sources and the energy transferred.

Electricity is generated using a number of different energy sources including coal, oil, gas, nuclear energy, wind and water. All of these are used to create movement. Conventional power stations use energy sources to create steam that turns giant turbines or generators. Wind and water turn the turbines directly and are more environmentally friendly. These generators work in the opposite way to electric motors in that they turn movement into electricity whereas a motor turns electricity into movement. Simply, electricity is produced in a wire when it moves in a magnetic field or when a nearby magnetic field is moved. Power station generators are huge and the magnetic coil or field in moving produces a current called an alternating current (AC). These are usually called alternators (smaller versions can be found in cars). In an

alternating current, the electrons go first in one direction and then in the opposite one. A generator that produces a direct current (DC) is usually called a dynamo. A direct current is one that always flows in the same direction.

Electricity is distributed using a system of high voltage cables carrying anything up to 400 000 volts. Since the output from a power station is 22 000 volts, a transformer is used to step up the voltage. Likewise our homes use 220–240 volts so transformers are again used to step down the voltage. Many items of electrical equipment in the home have similar step-down transformers to reduce the voltage to the required level.

Where mains electricity is not available or appropriate for safety or convenience reasons, batteries are used as a source of electrical energy. A **battery** really consists of two or more cells. A cell is the basic unit that produces electricity. Cells act a little like water pumps and push the electrons around a **circuit** of conductive material.

Science Fair CD-ROM (Sherston Software) offers activities that focus on Physical Processes at Key Stage 1 including electricity, sound and light.

Electromagnetic spectrum

Light travels in waves. These waves are just one of seven types of electromagnetic waves (waves of energy associated with electric and magnetic fields produced when atoms or electrons lose energy) that make up the electromagnetic spectrum. All electromagnetic waves travel through space at the same speed (the speed of light) and do not require a supporting medium in which to travel.

However, while all these waves travel at the same speed, their wavelengths and frequency vary since each carry different amounts of energy. The colours of the light spectrum (red, orange, yellow, green, blue, indigo and violet) are the only part of the electromagnetic spectrum that we can see, the rest are invisible. Infrared, microwave and radio waves all have longer wavelengths and carry less energy than visible light. Ultraviolet, X-ray and gamma rays have shorter wavelengths and carry more energy. All objects give off electromagnetic waves, from the largest solar body to the smallest speck on the earth, even our bodies.

Wave type	Wavelength	Properties	Uses
Gamma rays	1/100 000 000 mm	Emitted by radioactive materials Can destroy cells and cause mutations	Treating cancer Sterilisation of medical instruments and food
X-rays	1/1 000 000 mm	Absorbed by bones and teeth but passes through flesh Dangerous in high doses	Detecting broken bones, damaged teeth and diseases in the body
Ultraviolet rays	1/10 000 mm	Emitted by the Sun and other white-hot objects Will pass through air but not solids Can cause burning to the skin	Sterilising materials Sun beds Marking goods to deter theft

Wave type	Wavelength	Properties	Uses
Visible light	1/1000 mm	Light with differing wavelengths appears as different colours to us	Artificial lighting
Infrared rays	1/100 mm	Emitted by all warm/hot surfaces Can be detected by heat sensitive devices	Heating and cooking Tracking and locating objects at night, such as lost people
Microwaves	10 mm	Absorbed by some materials such as water Reflected by metals. Passes through materials such as glass, paper and plastic	Cooking and satellite communications
Radiowaves	10 000 m	Can be transmitted around the Earth	Carry radio, TV and communication signals

Electromagnetism

There are very many objects in everyday use that make use of electromagnetism, such as bells, electric motors, loudspeakers, audio and videotapes and computer disks. All electric currents produce a magnetic field, albeit a very small force. This effect can be increased by wrapping a coil of insulated wire around an iron core, such as a nail. When a current is passed through the wire, the iron nail becomes magnetised and a controllable **magnet** has been created since when the current is turned off the nail will lose its magnetic properties. Increasing the number of coils of wire around the iron core, or increasing the current being passed through the wire, can increase the strength of an electromagnet. Electromagnetism can be useful (e.g. in a car-breaker's yard) as the magnetism is controllable and can be switched on and off.

Electrons

Electrons are very tiny particles that orbit the nucleus of **atoms** in a similar way to the planets orbiting the Sun, and have a negative electrical charge. This negative charge of one electron balances out the positive charge of one proton.

Electrons are not solid objects but are bundles of energy that move at nearly the same speed as light. It is the flow of charge along a conductive material that is called an electric **current.**

The bonding of electrons from different atoms is characteristic of certain **materials**. For example, in salt atoms give away or take in electrons (**ionic bonding**), in water atoms share their electrons **(covalent bonding)** and in metals the electrons flow around all the atoms **(metallic bonding)**.

Elements

An element is a substance that consists entirely of atoms of only one type and is therefore one that cannot be broken down into any simpler substances. There are 92 naturally occurring elements with another 20 or so that scientists have made. Of the 92 that occur naturally, some are present on Earth in abundance, while others are comparatively rare. The most common elements in the universe as a whole are hydrogen and helium which together account for 98% of the matter that make up the stars. These together with the other elements were created as a result of the so-called 'Big Bang' that occurred when the Earth and planets were created thousands of millions of years ago.

Elements, then, are the building blocks for all other substances. Indeed every substance in the universe is made up from one or more of the elements. In the Earth's crust there is more oxygen than any other element. Together with silicon, it accounts for nearly 75% of the crust. In the human body, hydrogen, carbon and oxygen are the most common elements making up just over 97% of the body mass.

Elements can be sorted into two very simple groups depending upon their properties, metals and non-metals.

Property	Metal	Non-metal
State of matter	Usually solid at room temperature	Mostly gases at room temperature
Melting point	Usually high	Usually low
Boiling point	Usually high	Usually low
Conductivity	Good	Mostly poor

There are some non-metals which differ from the general rule, for example carbon and silicon.

Atoms of more than one element can make **mixtures** and **compounds**.

Endocrine system

The endocrine system controls and coordinates some functions and the working of some parts of the human body. By releasing hormones or chemical messengers from glands, the endocrine system is able to give instructions to target cells and organs for certain functions to be carried out.

The human body has over 50 different hormones: some are responsible for regulating various important substances in the body, while others control the way in which the body grows and develops. Some of the most important hormones and the glands that produce them are listed in the table below.

Gland	Hormone	Function
Pituitary	Produces many different hormones	To stimulate other glands to produce their own hormones
Thyroid	Thyroxine	To regulate growth and the rate that food is broken down
Pancreas	Produces hormones such as insulin and glucagons	To control sugar levels in the body
Adrenal	Adrenaline	To control heart and breathing rates
Ovaries	Oestrogen and progesterone	To control the onset of puberty, menstruation and ovulation in women
Testes	Testosterone	To control the onset of puberty and regulate the production of sperm in men

Energy

Energy is described as the capacity for doing work and is the thing that makes things happen. Without energy, nothing in the universe would happen and whenever energy is used **forces** are involved in starting things, moving them or stopping them.

While there are different types of energy, most of it can be traced back to the Sun. In fact, more energy reaches the Earth from the Sun in an hour than all of us use in a year.

Types of energy:

- *Chemical.* That part of the energy that is stored within an **atom** or **molecule** and is generally released by a chemical reaction. Radioactive materials release energy as they decay. Chemical energy is generally associated with food and fuels and is stored in the chemical make-up of some substances such as plants, oil, coal and batteries. The chemical changes that take place produce new substances and provide energy. For example, when we eat food, energy is released when the food is digested.

- *Kinetic.* The energy a body possesses when it is in motion. All moving things therefore have kinetic energy, which increases as the mass and speed of the object also increases. If the mass of a moving object is doubled, then its kinetic energy is also doubled. If its speed doubles, then its kinetic energy is quadrupled.

- *Potential.* The energy that an object possesses due to its position or the state it is in. Types of potential energy include:
    - *gravitational*: a ball at the top of a slope has potential energy because it is gravity that pulls it down the slope. The potential energy of an object increases as its mass and height of fall increase;
    - *elastic or strain*: an elastic band or spring has elastic potential energy when stretched or squashed;

- *electrical*: a battery makes electrical energy from a chemical reaction and therefore has electrical potential energy. It is also described as the ability of an electric current to do work;
- *magnetic*: a piece of iron near a magnet is said to have magnetic potential energy.

- **Heat**. When a substance or object is heated the molecules in the material move; the hotter the material the faster the molecules move. The moving molecules possess kinetic energy that can be used to do work.

- **Light**. Light energy is a form of electromagnetic radiation in the **electromagnetic spectrum.** Light energy from the Sun can be converted into electrical energy in a solar cell.

- **Sound**. Sound energy, because it involves the movement of waves, is a form of kinetic energy.

- **Nuclear**. Nuclear energy is the energy that is stored in the nuclei of all atoms. The energy is released in the form of heat and light when a nuclear reaction occurs as in a nuclear power station or a nuclear explosion.

Energy is measured in joules after the English scientist James Joule, who realised that work produces heat and that heat is a form of energy. Work is done when a force moves an object through a measured distance. The formulae used to measure this is:

Work (in joules) =
Force (in newtons) × distance moved in the direction of the force (in metres)

Therefore one **joule** is the work done when a force of one newton moves something a distance of one metre in the direction of the force.

Joules, and more especially kilojoules (kj), a thousand joules, are also used to measure the energy content of our food.

The energy that is required to carry out work is released from fuel sources. A **fuel** is a substance that is used for producing heat or kinetic energy, either through the release of its chemical energy during burning or its nuclear energy by nuclear fission.

Energy change and transfer

Just like matter, energy can be neither created nor destroyed; it can only be changed from one type to another (see **conservation of energy**). These energy changes or conversions are taking place all the time all around us, every day. When a lamp is turned on, electrical energy is changed into light and heat energy. When we eat, the chemical energy contained in our food is changed into sound energy when we speak or kinetic energy when we move something. These transfers of energy can be linked together to form energy chains. For example, it is possible to see that when we ride a bicycle we are expending, indirectly, energy from the Sun.

The Sun	Growing food	Eating food	Riding
Inside the Sun nuclear energy is converted into heat and light energy	Our food is largely plant based (animals are also fed on plants, see **food chains**). The plants convert light energy from the Sun into chemical energy during the process of **photosynthesis**	When we eat food the chemical energy it contains is transferred to our bodies to enable us to carry out activities	Riding a bicycle changes this chemical energy into potential and kinetic energy

During all processes of energy change and transfer some energy is lost. No transfers are 100% effective; many systems and machines are very inefficient with large amounts of energy not being used for its initial purpose but being lost. For example, when you drive a car a great deal of the energy obtained from the fuel is changed not into kinetic energy to make the car move, but into heat and sound energy. Similarly, when a lamp is lit only about 5% of the energy used is converted into light; the rest is lost as heat. A lamp, therefore, is said to have an energy efficiency of 5%. Manufacturers are constantly working to produce equipment that has a greater degree of energy efficiency, without any loss of performance.

Environment

There are rich and varied ranges of **habitats** in the world in which many different creatures live. The conditions and surroundings, both living and non-living, that exist in these habitats make up the environment. Creatures exploit their environment in order to survive. This means that an environment can be:

- a source of energy;
- a source of raw materials;
- a place to live and shelter;
- somewhere to deposit waste.

Unlike most animals, humans are able to change their environment in order to suit their way of living. This can, and does, often have an impact on other living things, both plants and animals, and not always for the better. Many people are becoming increasingly aware and concerned about the damage that some human activities can cause to the environment and the subsequent effects on other living things.

Evaporation

Evaporation is the process of converting a liquid into a vapour without the liquid necessarily reaching boiling point. The fastest moving **molecules** in the liquid acquire enough energy to allow them to escape from the surface of the liquid and to form a gas. The **kinetic energy** of the remaining molecules is reduced, therefore the process of evaporation causes a cooling in the liquid.

The process of evaporation occurs faster if the liquid is of a higher temperature. If water is heated to boiling point (100°C), evaporation will take place inside the liquid causing bubbles of water vapour to form and rise to the surface to escape, hence the bubbling of boiling water.

Evaporation also takes place from the surface of solids and can be observed when solids lose moisture and dry out. It can also be seen when drying clothes in the Sun and when drying your hair with a hair dryer. See also **states of matter**.

Evolutionary change

The theory of evolution suggests that the first living things on the Earth appeared over 3000 million years ago and were very simple single-celled creatures. Slowly, over millions of years, these simple creatures evolved into the many thousands of plants and animals that we see today. Much of the evidence for this theory has come from studying fossils, the remains of plants and animals that lived many years ago. These fossils were formed when the plants or animals died and were buried in a layer of mud. Over millions of years this became sedimentary rock. From studying fossils, scientists are able to determine when the plant or animal was actually alive and are able to build up a picture of the changes that they have undergone over time.

Charles Darwin is noted for carrying out much work in the area of evolution. In his book *The Origin of Species* he outlined a theory that he called natural selection. This theory contains three main ideas:

- **Variation** *within a species*. Within the same species there are many different individuals. The species of which humans are a part highlights this as we notice differences between people, such as height, weight, hair and skin colour. These differences occur for both genetic and environmental reasons.

- **Survival** *of the fittest*. Because of the variations within species, there is often a struggle among plants and animals for survival. Those that do survive are usually those that are the fittest, less likely to suffer diseases, able to avoid predators, able to compete successfully for resources such as space, shelter and food and able to adapt to differing climates. Those plants and animals that are able to survive are able to pass the 'survival characteristics' on to their offspring. This becomes a process called natural selection and leads to species developing and evolving in a particular way.

- **Adaptation** *of organisms*. The changes that take place within a species to allow it to survive are called adaptations and result from those individuals with the appropriate characteristics being more likely, and able, to reproduce.

Excretion and excretory system

All **living things** have to get rid of waste. This process is called excretion and

is important because a build up of waste produced as a result of processes that take place in the **cells** of an organism, such as **respiration**, can be poisonous. In humans, excretion is the output of these unwanted products such as carbon dioxide and water, which we excrete through our lungs. We also excrete nitrogen compounds, salts and water in our urine as well as salt and water when we sweat. Although it is often thought of as excretion, strictly speaking, excretion does not include the process whereby we get rid of undigested food as faeces. This is due to the fact that undigested food never passes through our cells.

Plants also need to get rid of waste. During the process of **photosynthesis**, plants release waste oxygen and carbon dioxide from their leaves. This usually takes place during the day since it is then that the rate at which photosynthesis takes place exceeds the rate of plant respiration. At night, photosynthesis does not take place so the plant then excretes carbon dioxide.

Fertilisation

Fertilisation is the process in sexual **reproduction** where a male gamete and a female gamete join together. Gametes are special reproductive cells which themselves are sexually differentiated. The female gametes are called egg cells or ova while the male gametes are called sperm. When the cells join during fertilisation, the fertilised cell is called a zygote. This develops into an embryo and a new individual of the species.

The fertilisation of a female gamete by a male can take place in one of two ways, depending on the species. In most land animals, fertilisation takes place internally (internal fertilisation), that is the sperm is passed from the male into the female's body. However, in some animals, notably fish and amphibians, the female lays unfertilised eggs for the male to pour his sperm over. This process is called external fertilisation. Most animals with external fertilisation produce many eggs so that enough will survive (some will be lost or eaten) to be fertilised.

Floating and sinking

Whether an object floats or sinks depends on the balance of the **forces** being exerted by the object and the liquid the object is in. When an object is placed in water, it exerts a downward force because of the effect of **gravity** on that object. There is, however, another force acting on the object that is opposing gravity: this force is exerted by the water and is called an upthrust. If the force of gravity is greater than the upthrust, then there will be a movement (unbalanced forces cause movement) and the object will sink. If, however, the upthrust is equal to the gravitational force, then the object will float. This upthrust is equal to the weight of the water that is displaced by the object. So if the weight of an object is equal to the weight of the water displaced, it will float. An object will sink if its weight is greater than the weight of water it displaces.

Two factors that affect this displacement are density and shape.

- The density of an object is simply how packed together the matter within the object is. A low-density material such as cork displaces enough water to provide an upthrust that is equal to its own weight, therefore it floats. A rock, on the other hand, is very dense and does not displace sufficient water to equal its weight and therefore sinks. In a similar way, ice floats because the density of ice is less than that of water.

- A block of plasticine placed in water will sink. If the same block of plasticine were to be made into a simple boat shape, it would float, because its shape (the overall volume includes the air within the boat shape) is now displacing an amount of water equal to its own mass.

Flowering plants
See **plants**

Food chains and webs

Plants and animals within an **ecosystem** rely on other **plants** and **animals** within that ecosystem for their food. The relationships between them can be seen in terms of a food chain or food web. An example of a food chain would be → plant → rabbit → fox, since a rabbit feeds on plants and a fox feeds on the rabbit. The fox together with all other animals are unable to produce their own food so need to seek food and are called **consumers**. Plants, however, do produce their own food so are called **producers**.

Animals often belong to several food chains since they eat several types of food. These food chains therefore combine to make food webs. A food web can include plants and animals from different ecosystems since some living things feed on both land and water. They are therefore part of several food chains. Within food chains and webs, there is much interdependence. A change in the numbers of one living thing can have an effect on other creatures.

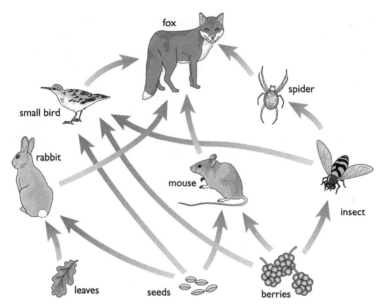

In the illustrations above, the direction of the arrows indicates the flow of energy.

Forces

Forces operate around us every day and while most are not immediately obvious their effects are plain to see. Quite simply, a force is a push or a pull. It is something that acts on an object and can have several effects. Forces can cause:

- a stationary object to start moving – e.g. the push on a toy car across the floor;
- a moving object to stop moving – e.g. the push exerted to stop the car moving;
- moving objects to speed up – e.g. that extra push to make the car go faster;
- moving objects to slow down – e.g. the push to slow it down again;
- moving objects to change direction – e.g. the push and pull of a steering wheel to avoid an obstacle;
- objects to change shape – e.g. the push to screw up a piece of paper.

There are a number of different types of forces:

- *contact forces* when two objects are pushed together – a contact force can be seen when you push yourself away from the side of a swimming pool or kick a ball;
- *electric forces* act between electrical charges – static electricity exerts an electric force;
- *frictional forces* act to try to prevent movement – they cause **friction**, which stops objects slipping. The brakes on a bicycle use friction to stop the bicycle moving;

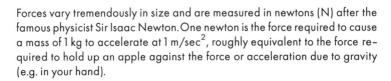

- *gravitational forces* are those caused by the pull of objects on others as the Earth's **gravity** pulls us towards the Earth;
- *magnetic forces* act on magnetic materials — some door catches are magnetic and pull objects together using **magnetism**.

Forces vary tremendously in size and are measured in newtons (N) after the famous physicist Sir Isaac Newton. One newton is the force required to cause a mass of 1 kg to accelerate at 1 m/sec^2, roughly equivalent to the force required to hold up an apple against the force or acceleration due to gravity (e.g. in your hand).

Many objects are acted upon by more than one force. When this occurs the overall result of the two forces is called the resultant force. This resultant force has the same effect as the two combined forces. If two equal forces were acting on an object at the same angle, the resultant force would act between the two. For example, if two equal forces were simultaneously pulling an object North and East, the resultant force would make the object move Northeast. If, however, two different forces were acting on the object, then the resultant force would be in the direction of the stronger force. That is, if there is a larger force pulling the object South and a smaller force pulling North, the resultant force would move the object to the South.

Forces acting in opposite directions can be called equal and opposite forces depending on their size. If they were to be equal, then the forces are balanced and no movement, or change in movement if the body is already moving, would take place. If, however, there was a larger force, then the forces would be unbalanced and movement would occur. For example, if two tug of war teams were equally matched and exerted the same force then the rope would stay in the same position. The forces would cancel each other out giving a resultant force of zero.

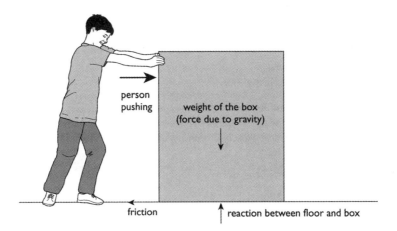

person pushing

weight of the box (force due to gravity)

friction

reaction between floor and box

Free electrons

An electron that is not attached to an atom, molecule or ion but is free to move about is called a free electron. The effects of the movement of free electrons can be observed in the flow of **electricity** and the conduction of **heat** through a solid.

Freezing point

The freezing point of a liquid is the temperature at which the liquid begins to change from a liquid to a solid. When a liquid cools, the particles that are moving slow down until they lock together forming a solid.

Friction

Friction is a force that opposes motion. Friction occurs because, despite their looks, no surfaces are actually perfectly smooth. At a microscopic level, surfaces show ridges which inhibit movement. At a molecular level, molecules can be attracted and try to catch or stick the surfaces together resulting in a slowing of movement between the surfaces.

Friction can be a very useful force. The friction between the wheels of a car or bicycle on a dry road enables us to go forward without skidding and friction between the brakes and the wheel rims enables us to stop. Friction between ice skates and skis produces enough heat to temporarily melt the ice under the skates. Thus skaters and skiers travel on a thin film of water without which skates and skis would stick to the ice.

Friction can also be a hindrance to movement in moving machine parts, such as the gear wheels on a bicycle, which is why we use lubricants to reduce this friction.

Friction has three major effects.

- It slows moving objects down or prevents them moving completely.
- It produces heat when a force is applied. The moving surfaces heat up when there is movement between them.
- It causes surfaces to wear as they move together.

These effects can be reduced by:

- using smoother surfaces;
- reducing the pressure between two surfaces;
- using lubricants to create a smooth film between the surfaces effectively keeping them apart;
- reducing the area of the surfaces in contact with each other.

Conversely the effects of friction can be increased by:

- using rougher surfaces;
- increasing the pressure between two surfaces;
- using materials that are less likely to easily slide together.

Friction also affects movement through the air and again slows down movement. This force is called **air resistance**. There is also some resistance caused by friction as an object moves through water.

Fuels

A fuel is a substance that is used for producing heat energy, either through the release of its chemical energy during burning or its nuclear energy by nuclear fission. The burning or combustion of fuels is used in many ways in homes and industry and in the generation of electricity. Fossil fuels (which are mostly hydrocarbons: compounds of hydrogen and carbon) such as coal, oil and gas are some of the most important and widely used fuels. As they burn, the hydrogen and carbon react with oxygen to produce water, carbon dioxide and heat.

Fossil fuels are so called because they are just that, fossils. Millions of years ago, the Earth was a vastly different place, covered with huge forests and oceans full of organisms. These plants and animals gradually died off and decayed. They were subsequently covered over by both the sea and sediment or by rocks. This caused the decaying matter to be compressed and, over millions of years, oil was formed from the sea creatures and coal from the plant life.

Heat from fossil fuels can be utilised in very many ways. One of the main uses is for the generation of electricity.

Galaxies

The **Universe** is made up of billions of stars that are grouped together into enormous collections called galaxies. Astronomers believe that, on average, a galaxy contains in the region of 100 billion stars and is about 100 000 light years (see **years and light years**) in diameter and that there are about 100 000 million galaxies, of which our own galaxy, the Milky Way, is but just one. The Milky Way is spiral in shape (galaxies can be spiral, elliptical or irregular in shape), rotates about a central point and contains about 200 000 million stars, with our **Sun** being one of them.

Galaxies are not stationery and, like all galaxies, the Milky Way is continually moving about in space. It takes the Sun about 220 million years to make one circuit around its central point in the Milky Way.

Gases
See **states of matter**

Genes

All different species of life, whether they are plants or animals, have a number of very unique characteristics that make them what they are. These characteristics are carried from generation to generation in a code, a set of very clear instructions, that allow for the reproduction and continuation of that species. This code is carried in molecules of **DNA** and is extremely complex. The code inside one human cell contains between 50 000 and 100 000 separate instructions called genes and each gene controls a different characteristic.

Sometimes a single gene controls a characteristic, such as hair colour, but more usually several genes are involved. Often a pair of genes, one from the mother and one from the father, control a characteristic. Normally, one of the pair is dominant and the other is recessive and the dominant one will mask the effects of the recessive one so that the dominant gene will determine the particular characteristic. These characteristics are known as phenotypes and the genetic make up of an individual is known as the genotype.

Knowledge of genes allows us to explain how characteristics are passed from one generation to the next and also to predict characteristics in that next generation. We can, therefore, determine the eye colour of a baby by studying the genes of the parents (in genetics, a dominant gene is represented by a capital letter and a lower case letter represents a recessive gene). If a male with brown eyes (genotype BB) were to father a child to a female with blue eyes (genotype bb) then the baby's genotype would be Bb since the male's genes are, in this case, the dominant ones. However there are three possible genotypes for eye colour: BB, Bb and bb. The genotypes BB and Bb will both give a brown-eyed baby whereas genotype bb would give a blue-eyed baby. Using this representation of genes, it is possible to predict what will happen when parents with other eye colour genotypes have children.

Knowledge of genetics is also helpful in the diagnosis and treatment of hereditary diseases such as cystic fibrosis and haemophilia.

Giant structures

A giant structure is an arrangement of atoms that are held together by attractive charges of positively and negatively charged ions. This bonding, which is ionic bonding, makes a new substance that is very strong and therefore difficult to break apart. Diamonds are examples of giant structures.

Gravity

Gravity is a non-contact **force**. It is a force that pulls things closer together. The force of gravitational attraction between two objects depends upon the distance between them and their mass. All objects have this gravitational attraction, though when the two masses are small, the effects are relatively negligible. Perhaps the most common force we are familiar with is gravity, the force that keeps our feet on the ground wherever we stand. If we jump up, or drop something, the force of the Earth's gravity returns us to the ground and causes the object to fall. The gravitational force on the Earth is sufficiently strong to hold our atmosphere in place without which there would not be life on our planet.

However, the Earth itself is subject to a gravitational attraction. The Sun, which contains 99.8% of the mass of our Solar System, exerts a very strong gravitational force as its gravity holds the Earth and the other planets in the **Solar System** in their orbits. The Moon also has a gravitational attraction but because it is much smaller than the Earth, its gravity is less than that of the Earth. Even so, the Moon's gravitational force on the Earth causes the oceans to move. Tides are associated with where the Moon is relative to a particular body of water on the Earth. Furthermore, when the Moon and Sun are in alignment, the overall gravitational force on the oceans is increased, causing higher **tides**. The lower size and gravitational force on the Moon means that falling objects accelerate downwards at one-sixth of the rate they do on Earth and you could jump six times higher on the Moon than on Earth.

When objects fall to the ground due to gravity, they accelerate at the same rate even though they may be of different masses. If you were to drop a cricket ball and a tennis ball at the same time, they would both reach the ground at the same time, despite the fact that the cricket ball clearly has a greater mass. This assumes that we ignore any variations in **air resistance** that may be acting on each ball. This happens because a force is required to make the objects accelerate towards the ground. The force of gravity acting on the cricket ball, however, is greater than the gravitational force acting upon the tennis ball since the cricket ball has a greater mass. Once the **acceleration** has taken place both balls will be travelling at the same speed and will therefore hit the ground at the same time. Put simply, the larger mass requires a larger force to get it going at a particular **velocity**. All objects therefore, unless subject to other forces, accelerate to the ground due to gravity at 9.8 m/s^2.

Growth

Most living things grow as they go through the various stages of their development. This is due to the division and increase in numbers of cells. When a cell reaches a certain size, it first copies itself, and then these two new cells begin to divide. This cell division continues as long as the living thing is growing.

In humans, this cell division, and therefore growth, does not always occur at the same rate. As a human baby grows and develops into a child and then an adult, the cells in parts of the body such as the limbs grow at a faster rate than those in the head. The result is not just a growth in body size but also a change in body shape. Hormones, chemicals that are carried in the blood around the body, largely control this growth and development. These hormones control the rate of growth, so that, for example, when a child reaches 11 or 12 years of age, there are quicker and significant periods of growth and change. Humans go through clearly identifiable stages of growth until cell division virtually comes to a halt.

Stages of development	Approximate age range	Characteristics
Baby	0–1	Large head, short arms and legs
Toddler	1–3	Longer arms and legs, muscle growth to enable walking
Child	3–11	Stronger muscles to allow walking and running
Adolescent	11–18	Limbs grown much more, fine motor skills more coordinated, speed of growth greater
Adult	18+	Most human adults now fully grown, the head is now a relatively smaller part of the body

Whereas humans continue growing until they reach adulthood and then, apart from weight changes, growth stops, many plants grow continually throughout their lives, both in height and bulk. A tree, for example, grows in two different ways. The cells at the tips of the roots and branches divide so that they grow longer, meanwhile the cells under the bark divide to make both the trunk and branches thicker.

Habitats

A habitat is a place where a community of organisms live. A habitat can only support plants and animals that are adapted to its conditions and then only in limited numbers. This is due to the competition that exists between, and within, species for food. The group of plants and animals living in a habitat is called a community and within the habitat all their needs are provided for, ranging from food and water to shelter.

Changes can and do occur in habitats. These can be climatic and affect the supply of food or the provision of shelter. Animals and plants living in a habitat as a community are also part of **food chains** and consequently a food web. Such changes can have devastating effects upon the community and ultimately change the nature of the habitat as species that feed on particular plants or animals find that their food supply is no longer available. This can lead to animals moving, dying or adapting their eating habits.

Habitats are often changed, not by other environmental or climatic factors but by the intervention and action of humans. As we continue to use the land and oceans we too are affecting habitats, sometimes by accident or negligence, other times on purpose as we seek to develop and build on particular areas of land.

Habitats (Espresso Productions) covers five different habitats and is appropriate for teaching and learning at Key Stage 2.

Harmful substances

Harmful substances affect all living things in many different ways. It is important therefore that if the human body is to be kept in a safe and healthy condition then care and consideration needs to be given to the effects certain substances can have on the body. Substances that can cause both long- and short-term harm include tobacco, alcohol and drugs. These substances can seriously damage and affect the central nervous system of the body, together with other systems and organs.

- Tobacco causes harm, when smoked, by:
    - increasing the production of mucus that is meant to clean the lungs. However, smoking also slows down the cleaning effect resulting in a build-up in the bronchioles causing the typical 'smoker's cough';
    - allowing germs to get into the lungs more easily as a result of the slower cleaning process;

- causing the bronchioles to become narrower, reducing the surface area of alveoli which can absorb oxygen in the lungs which results in breathing difficulties;
- increasing the chances of developing lung cancer.

- Alcohol cause harm to the body, by:
    - acting as a depressant that slows down the reactions in the nervous system;
    - affecting the brain leading to a reduction of inhibitions and a boost to confidence. This can result in uncontrollable and violent behaviour;
    - causing damage to the liver and the brain;
    - causing dehydration.

- Drugs that are taken for non-medical reasons, i.e. not medicines, can be dangerous to the body by:
    - damaging the organs of the body – drugs such as cannabis can damage brain cells; solvents can damage the kidney and liver as well as the brain;
    - leading to addiction – taking most drugs becomes habitual. This can lead to addiction and a dependence on drugs where people begin to suffer from headaches, depression and sickness unless they have regular quantities of the drug;
    - impairing behaviour – people addicted to and abusing drugs often behave in unusual and irrational ways as they experience a whole range of emotions as the drugs take effect.

There are four types of drugs which affect the body: some are used as **medicines,** others for recreation:

- *Sedatives*. These slow down the brain and make people sleepy and include Valium, barbiturates and alcohol.

- *Stimulants*. These cause the brain to speed up making people more alert. They include ecstasy and cocaine. Coffee, tea and some fizzy drinks also contain the mild stimulant caffeine. Tobacco also contains the stimulant nicotine.

- *Hallucinogens*. Tthese cause people to experience things that are not real; they hallucinate. Marijuana and LSD are hallucinogens.

- *Painkillers*. These take away the sense of pain that people may suffer and include paracetamol, morphine and heroin.

DrugSense CD-ROM (New Media Press Ltd) is appropriate for use in Key Stage 2. It consists of a CD-ROM and a teacher's manual.

Health

All **living things**, both **plants** and **animals**, carry out a number of **life processes** that are common characteristics of living things. A plant's or animal's ability to carry out these processes is dependent on the health of that living thing. It is important that plants and animals remain healthy in order to perform their various functions. As humans health affects both the quality and length of our life; similarly, with plants — an unhealthy plant is likely to die prematurely. If humans use that plant for food, then it is in their interest to maintain healthy plants (crops).

Healthy humans

There are a number of key factors that determine human health.

- *Food.* The human body needs an adequate supply of food to maintain a good level of health. It is important that humans eat a **balanced diet**.

- *Water.* The human body is about 65% water so it is important for the effective functioning of the body systems and organs that we drink sufficient amounts of water.

- *Oxygen.* The human body needs to take in oxygen so that the process of cellular respiration can take place. This is called aerobic respiration because it involves oxygen. Food substances (mainly glucose from carbohydrates) are combined with the oxygen resulting in the release of energy into the body.

- *Heat.* The human body has a temperature of 37°C, which remains constant unless the body is ill. During cellular **respiration**, energy is released around the body, some of which is in the form of heat. This occurs at the same time as the body is losing heat. If there is a net loss of heat, the body responds by shutting off some blood vessels near the surface of skin and making body hair stand up. If there is a net gain in heat, then the body produces sweat as a means of cooling down. The human body continues to operate in the extremes of atmospheric temperatures but once these become too hot or cold, the responses of the brain and nervous system begin to change and judgements and reactions are affected.

- *Exposure to harmful substances.* **Harmful substances** can very seriously damage the body and its systems, and can lead to illness, accident or death.

- *Exercise and rest.* Regular exercise and rest are important factors in maintaining good health. Exercise can benefit the heart (making it stronger and helping to eliminate the build-up of fatty deposits in the arteries), keep muscles and joints in good condition and give a feeling of overall well-being. Rest is important because it gives the body the time to carry out its basic functions of repair and maintenance. Lack of sufficient sleep can lead to a hormonal imbalance in the body which can result in stress, anxiety and the inability to make clear and considered judgements.

- *Safety.* It is important that, as humans, we take every possible precaution to keep ourselves safe. This involves assessing the possible risks involved in carrying out the very many activities that humans do. People will often decide that the risks involved range from the minimal to the very real, and take appropriate decisions to ensure their safety. Others may choose to ignore any potential risks and risk injury or death through carrying out a particular activity.

- *Freedom from disease.* Humans have worked tirelessly in seeking solutions to many medical problems, including diseases, through the development of **medicines** and vaccines. Vaccination is one way of avoiding a disease and involves introducing a weak **micro-organism** into the body. This causes the body to develop antibodies that act to prevent the disease developing in the body. The antibodies remain in the body so if the person is in contact later with a full-blown version of the disease, the antibodies quickly replicate themselves to prevent the disease developing to a harmful level. Vaccinations have successfully prevented many diseases from becoming widespread and have contributed to the overall health of humans.

Healthy plants

For continued good health plants need:

- *A safe and suitable place to germinate and grow.* Plants need a good medium, a well aerated and nutrient rich soil for example, in which to grow. This enables the plant to put down a root system that is sufficient to anchor it into place and to provide the means of collecting appropriate nutrients from the soil. The plant also needs sufficient space in which to grow and develop where it is not in danger from damage by the elements or other living things that may feed on it.

- *Water.* A good supply of water is essential to maintain growth and to carry out the process of **photosynthesis**. Plants also need water to help them maintain their shape and to keep them upright. Most water obtained by a plant comes through its root system although the leaves of the plant take in a small amount.

- *Oxygen and carbon dioxide.* Oxygen and carbon dioxide are both taken in by the plant through small pores, called stomata, on the underside of the plant's leaves. The carbon dioxide and water react to provide glucose and oxygen during **photosynthesis**.

- *Light from the Sun.* Sunlight, a source of **energy**, is essential in the process of photosynthesis.

- *Heat.* There is an optimum temperature range in which plants grow and flourish best. This obviously varies between species, as certain plants are more suited to particular climates. These temperatures range from 6°C to 40°C but most plants grow more profusely in higher temperatures. This occurs because the chemical reactions that take place in the plant's cell structure are speeded up when the temperature is raised. This can be observed in warm tropical rain forests where the plant growth is great.

- *Freedom from disease.* Just like humans, plants too suffer from the effects of diseases. Bacteria, viruses and fungi, known collectively as pathogens (a pathogen is an organism that causes disease), can be transmitted to plants through the air or soil. Animals can also transmit bacteria and viruses. These infections are often not treatable and lead to the death of the infected plant.

- *Freedom from consumers.* Plants are very often food for animals. These herbivores (plants eaters) are consumers within a **food chain** or food web and get their energy from eating the plant. While some plants grow sufficiently to sustain and meet the needs of the consumer, others are eaten in such a way that the plant suffers, for example from the eating of all its leaves, and subsequently withers and dies. Humans grow plants specifically for food, some of which are cropped (as in fruit trees) while others, such a grain crops, are harvested and the entire plant dies.

Heat

Heat is a form of energy. When a material is heated, it gains energy and its particles vibrate and move faster. This occurs when there is a difference in the temperature and heat is transferred to the material. The energy that the material gains is called thermal energy and can cause:

- the material (solid, liquid or gas) to change its state by melting, boiling or evaporating;
- the material to expand;
- the burning of the material.

Heat can be transferred in one of four ways.

1. *Conduction* is the transfer of heat energy through a solid material from places of higher temperature to places of lower temperature without the movement of the material. This is achieved by the movement of **free electrons** or by the collision of the molecules which make up the material. Free electron conduction is usually found in materials that are good conductors of heat, such as metals, and occurs comparatively quickly. Conduction through collision is much slower and is characteristic of poorer thermal conductors.

2. *Convection* is the transfer of heat by the movement of a gas or liquid. Electric convector heaters work in this way. Air is heated and expands, thereby becoming less dense which causes it to rise. As it rises, cooler air

takes its place and it too in turn is heated. Currents are set up which maintain a continuous process. Hot water systems work on this same principle.

3. *Evaporation* occurs as particles move away from the surface of a liquid and into the air as a gas.

4. *Radiation* is the transfer of energy by means of electromagnetic waves where no material is present to carry the heat. Heat transferred by radiation can be felt as the Sun's heat or as heat from a fire or radiator.

Heat is measured in joules which tell us how much thermal energy there is in a material or body.

Sometimes, however, we wish to prevent heat transfer taking place. Some materials are very good **thermal conductors** whilst others are very poor and are called **insulators**. Air is a very poor conductor of heat and therefore makes an excellent insulator. Many materials, which trap air, are used as insulation both by humans and naturally among birds and animals. We keep ourselves warm by wearing clothes, not to warm us up but to insulate our bodies and prevent heat loss. Layers of clothes effectively trap air around our bodies and prevent or reduce heat lost through convection. This trapped air also acts as a layer of insulation as it too is warmed with heat from our bodies.

Human body

The human body is an incredibly complex organism that not only carries out the life processes common to living things but also has a highly developed ability to make decisions and to carry out actions. No other living thing has developed in the same way, and to the same extent, as humans. The human body has a number of **body systems** that help the body to maintain itself, grow, develop and reproduce. There are also a number of organs that are key to the health and maintenance of the body. These are listed in the table below.

Organ	Function
Brain	The brain, which at birth contains about 1000 billion nerve cells, is part of the central **nervous system** and is divided into three main regions: • the brain stem and cerebellum take care of the body's functions such as circulation and breathing; • the cerebrum is much larger and processes information received via the **senses** by the peripheral **nervous system**.
Heart	The heart is part of the **circulatory system** and is a large **muscle** that pumps blood around the body. The heart is similar to two pumps working side by side: one pumps blood from the body to the lungs; the other pumps blood from the lungs and circulates it around the body.
Lungs	The lungs are often regarded as part of the **respiratory system**. They allow the body to breathe in air in order to take from it the oxygen that the body needs and to exhale the waste gases that are produced during the actual process of cellular **respiration**.

Organ	Function
Liver	The liver produces a green liquid called bile. This is used in the **digestive system**. It also stores glucose, vitamins and minerals as well as removes poisons that are in the blood. The **chemical reactions** that take place in the liver are exothermic; the heat produced is circulated around the body by the blood.
Kidneys	The kidneys are the main cleaning system within the body and are responsible for filtering the blood and removing waste substances. They also remove water from the digestive system.
Stomach	When food reaches the stomach it is broken down by the muscular action of the stomach and the gastric juices released by the stomach. These juices include hydrochloric acid and various enzymes.
Small intestines	Here food is broken down even further and nutrients pass into the bloodstream through the lining of the intestine.
Large intestines	Undigested food, water and fibre form faeces, which is then passed out of the body.

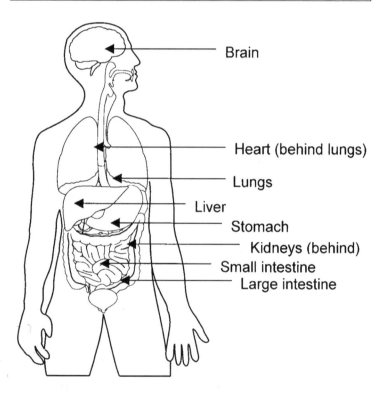

Bodywise CD-ROM (Sherston Software) is an interactive database of the human body that takes the children in Key Stage 2 on an informative journey deep into the human body.

Humidity

Humidity is a measure of the water vapour that is present in the air and may be given in terms of relative humidity (the amount of water vapour in the air compared to the maximum it can hold at that temperature) or absolute humidity (the number of grams of water in a cubic metre of air). If the **weather** is very humid, then the air is carrying a lot of water vapour. This is usually associated with warm temperature since warm air is able to hold more water vapour than cooler air. Humidity can be measured using a hygrometer. If it reaches more 100%, then the air is unable to carry any more water vapour and it will condense back into water and form clouds. See also **water cycle**.

Immune system

The **human body** and other organisms use their immune system as a means of staying healthy by fighting germs. **Micro-organisms** thrive in conditions that are warm and offer a supply of food; the human body offers such conditions. Many of the germs that get into the body are attacked by white blood cells, others by antibodies produced by the immune system. When attacked by a particular bacterium, if the body has encountered it before, the relevant antibodies recognise it and quickly replicate themselves to kill the invading cells. This happens when the human body has built up immunity to a particular bacterium.

Insulators

There are two types of insulators: electrical insulators and heat insulators. Insulators are materials that do not conduct either **heat** or **electricity**. Some **materials**, such as wood and plastic, are good insulators while others, such as metal, are poor. Materials that are good insulators do not have any **free electrons** to pass energy along so this takes place by vibration and the direct contact of **atoms**. Many such materials are not particularly dense and have air trapped within the material. Since air is not a good **conductor** of heat the material has good insulation properties.

Heat insulators are useful materials and serve a number of purposes:

- *Keeping our bodies warm*. Insulators allow us to prevent the transfer of heat away from our bodies. Clothes 'keep us warm', not by generating any heat energy but by slowing down the transfer of heat from our body into its surroundings.

- *Keeping our homes warm*. Insulators allow us to prevent heat being lost from our homes. For example, we put good thermal insulation materials in the walls and roofs of houses and install double-glazing.

Electrical insulators also serve a number of purposes:

- *Safety*. Materials that do not conduct **electricity** allow us to handle electrical equipment relatively safely since the **current** does not 'pass out' of the equipment and through the user.

- *Control*. Insulators allow us to control the flow of electricity around a circuit.

Invertebrate

An invertebrate is an animal with no backbone, although the description 'without a central nervous system' may be a more accurate one. Invertebrates make up about 97% of the animal species on Earth with many having soft bodies and living in water. In the animal kingdom, the **classification** of living things as invertebrates is an informal one in that it is not biologically accurate because it contains species from many unrelated phyla.

Ionic bonding

An ionic bond occurs when an atom of a metallic element loses or gains one or more of the electrons in its outer shell to the outer shell of a non-metallic element. In the process, each atom becomes electrically charged and is called an ion. The attraction between the two ions is very strong making ionic bonds very difficult to break. Compounds formed through ionic bonding are usually **solids** and will only melt at very high temperatures. When sodium and chlorine atoms form an ionic bond, for example, they become the **compound** sodium chloride (common salt).

Joules

A joule is a unit measure of energy and a measure of work. One joule is the work done when a force of one newton moves something a distance of 1 m in the direction of the force. Kilojoules (kJ) — 1000 joules — is a measure of the energy in food. Males and females of various ages use different levels of energy each day, depending on their activities and life style.

Kinetic energy

See **energy**

Life cycles

A life cycle is the process and stages of development that living things go through from the beginning to the end of their lives. Examples of life cycles from animals and plants are listed in the tables below.

Human Life Cycle		
Stage	**Approximate age**	**Characteristics**
Conception*	9 months prior to birth	Foetus develops in mother's womb.
Baby	0–1 year	Complete dependence on adults for feeding, moving and learning.
Toddler	1–3 years	Begins to become more independent, able to walk, feed and talk.
Child	3–11 years	Independence develops further, both physically and mentally. Able to dress themselvs. Begins and develops educational skills and attends formal schooling.
Adolescent	11–18 years	Educational developments continue as changes begin to take place physically and mentally during puberty — a transitional stage between childhood and adulthood.

Adult	18+ years	Physically and mentally well developed. Sexually developed with the ability to reproduce (occurs also during adolescence). Totally independent from parents with responsibilities for children, the community and family members.
Old age	65/70+	Mobility and health may begin to suffer. Dependence on others may increase again as a result of illness or incapacity.
Death	Anytime	While most humans live into old age, significant numbers die at what might be termed 'an early age' due to: • illness; • unhealthy life style; • accident; • injury.

*There is often disagreement over when human life begins, at conception or birth. However, conception is clearly part of the whole life cycle process.

Flowering Plant Life Cycle	
Stage	**Characteristics**
Seed germination	Seeds contain the DNA blueprint for the whole plant and are dispersed from the parent plant where they begin to grow.
Growth	Shoots and roots appear from the seed and small plants (seedlings) establish themselves. The plant continues to grow and develop, some over a very short period (months) and others over many years.
Pollination and fertilisation	Seeds within a plant are produced as a result of the joining together of pollen (the male cells) of a flower with the ovules (female egg cells). At this point fertilisation takes place. See **pollination** for more details.
Seed production and dispersal	Once fertilised the ovule develops into an embryo plant or seed. These are dispersed away from the parent plant in many different ways. The seed then begins to grow and develop into a new plant as the process of germination occurs. See also **seed dispersal**.
Death	Some plants die after one year of growth (annuals), others undergo a two-year life cycle (biennial). Some plants continue to grow, develop and reproduce for many years (perennials). Plant death can also occur at anytime due to illness.

Life processes

Living things can be separated from non-living things by considering what processes they go through in order to be considered living. These life processes are shared to a greater or lesser extent by all living things, be they animals or plants. Each of these life processes, **movement, reproduction, sensitivity, growth, respiration, excretion** and **nutrition** (MRS GREN) is dealt with in detail elsewhere. The table below summarises them.

Life process	Animals	Plants
Movement	Animals can move all or part of their bodies and from place to place.	Plants move in response to a stimulus such as light. They do not move from place to place.
Reproduction	Animals produce young.	New plants grow from seed or from parts of the parent plant.
Sensitivity	Animals notice and respond to stimuli in their surroundings.	Plants grow towards the light and respond to day length and to chemicals in the plants and the environment.
Growth	Animals usually stop growing when they reach adulthood.	Plants continue to grow as long as they live.
Respiration	Animals use oxygen to turn food into usable energy.	Plants use oxygen to turn food into usable energy.
Excretion	Waste substances such as food remains, gases and chemicals need to be removed from animal's bodies.	Plants need to get rid of waste gases and water.
Nutrition	Animals eat plants or other animals to give them energy.	Plants make their own food using carbon dioxide, energy from the sun and water.

Light

Light is a form of **energy** and can come from any number of different sources. These light sources are often called primary and secondary light sources. Primary light sources include things such as electrical lamps, candles and fires. The primary light source from which we get most of our light here on Earth is the Sun. Secondary light sources are those objects which reflect light towards us and can include things like the Moon, which, although it often lightens a dark night, is actually only reflecting light from the Sun.

Light travels in wave form and very fast – in fact, nothing travels faster. In a vacuum, light travels at a speed of 300 000 km (186 000 miles) per second. Outside a vacuum, its speed varies as it passes through different materials and **refraction** occurs. The light from the Sun takes about eight minutes to reach the Earth while light from the nearest star takes around four years. Light allows us to see the objects that are all round us, and their **colour**. When an object blocks the passage of light a shadow is formed.

When light from a light source reaches an object it can be:

- transmitted or allowed to travel through, like glass;
- absorbed, as in a black surface;
- reflected (see **reflection**), as in a smooth shiny surface like a mirror.

Materials that allow light to be transmitted fall into one of three groups.

1. Transparent materials such as glass allow most light that hits them to travel through in a relatively unchanged way. This allows us to see objects at

the other side of the material. Some of the light, however, is reflected from the material, which is why we are able to see the material or object from which it is made.

2. Translucent materials such as frosted glass or thin paper allow light through but the light is scattered as it passes through the material. This means that we are unable to see clearly through the material although we may be able to make out the presence of an object, its shape or colour.

3. Opaque materials, such as wood or rock, do not transmit any light at all. Instead, the light is either reflected or absorbed by the material. The reflected light is scattered and allows us to see the material and other objects around and about.

Some materials are particularly poor reflectors of light and absorb most of the light and heat energy that reaches them. Dark coloured materials absorb both light and heat and are therefore not suitable colours to wear in warm weather. Light coloured materials on the other hand do reflect both light and therefore heat and are more suitable for warm weather.

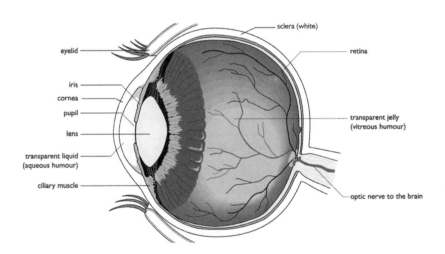

It is reflected light that allows us to see. Light from a light source is reflected from that object and enters our eyes. As it does so, an inverted image of the object is formed on the retina at the back of the eye. This produces an electrical impulse and a signal is sent along the optic nerve to the brain where this image is interpreted. We can only see objects when some light is present. In the total absence of light, absolute pitch black, we would not see anything even if it were directly in front of us.

While our ability to see is most remarkable and our eyes allow us to see objects that are many millions of kilometres away, such as stars, we cannot see things that are literally round the corner. Light appears to travel in straight lines, so that if an opaque object is between us and the light source, the light is reflected off it and does not reach our eyes. Hence our inability to see objects that are round corners. Surfaces that reflect light best are those that are smooth and shiny. Rougher, matt surfaces still reflect some light but some of it is also scattered. See **reflection** for more details.

Light varies in its intensity. A light source that transfers large amounts of energy in the form of light will produce light with a greater intensity or brightness. This can be seen clearly in waveform. The two waves below both have the same wavelength but different amplitudes. The first wave represents a light of low intensity or brightness, the second wave has high **amplitude** and therefore is of high intensity or brightness.

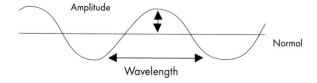

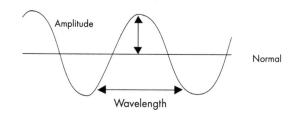

While the amplitude of a light wave determines the energy level of the light and therefore brightness, the wavelength of a light wave determines the nature of the actual light. Different colours of visible light have different wave lengths. The **colour** red, for example, has a shorter wavelength than yellow which in turn is shorter than violet. These colours are part of the colour spectrum which in turn is part of the **electromagnetic spectrum**.

The Met Office (http://www.meto.gov.uk/education/curriculum/leaflets/rainbows.html) offers online resources for teaching children at Key Stage 1 and 2 including worksheets and classroom activities for teaching about light through a topic on rainbows.

Lightning
See **static electricity**

Liquids
See **states of matter**

Living things

In order to begin to make sense of the world, we can separate everything into two simple groups: living things and non-living things. Living things can be described as those things that exhibit signs of carrying out **life processes** of **movement, reproduction, sensitivity, growth, respiration, excretion** and **nutrition** (MRS GREN). However, this definition can lead to confusion and disagreement since some objects, such as a fire, exhibit some of these characteristics and so it is also worth considering putting things into one of three groups:

- living;
- not living;
- never lived.

Consideration may also need to be given not only to the object but also to the raw materials from which it was made. It could be argued that a sheet of newspaper has never lived but the raw material that is used to produce the sheet of newspaper, wood pulp, did once live: as a tree. In that way, it would be possible to see that materials that once lived can be manufactured into objects that we then determine as having never lived. However, one thing that is clear is that all things, whether living things, plants or animals, large or small, are made of **cells**. These cells in turn are built up from **atoms** and **molecules** all of which can be seen as part of a much bigger picture.

Atoms come together to form:

- **molecules** (such as proteins). These join together to form
- **cells** (such as blood cells). Similar cells group to make
- **tissues** (such as muscle and bone tissue). These tissues form
- **organs** (such as the heart or brain) which work together as
- **systems** (such as the nervous system or circulatory system) within
- **organisms** (plants or animals). The same species of such organisms become
- **populations** (fish in a pond or birds in a woodland) which then live together with other populations as
- **communities** (all the species in a woodland) in particular habitats to form
- **ecosystems** (a community of organisms that interact with each other).

Magnetism

Magnetism is a property of materials that have the ability to attract iron, cobalt, nickel or their alloys such as steel, nichrome and Alnico. Magnets themselves are usually made from iron, cobalt and nickel or their alloys such as steel. It is, however, possible to incorporate these magnetic metals into other non-magnetic materials such as plastics. All magnets, whatever their shape, have two poles, north and south. These are created when the magnet is made. Magnetic materials have a number of 'miniature magnets' called domains, each themselves having a north and south pole. In a non-magnetised piece of metal, these domains are all jumbled up and their magnetic effects are cancelled out by each other. If the domains are all aligned, the overall effect becomes quite powerful and magnetism is produced.

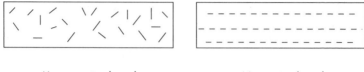

Unmagnetised steel   Magnetised steel

The end that the north pole of the domains point to becomes the north pole of the magnet and the other end becomes the south pole. These names are used since the domains are attracted to the North and South poles of the Earth, which in itself is like a huge magnet with a magnetic field around it. The iron core at the centre of the Earth causes this field. The Northern Hemisphere of the Earth, however, has a south magnetic pole and the Southern Hemisphere a north magnetic pole. As unlike poles attract, the North pole of a compass is attracted to the south magnetic pole of the Arctic.

While magnets attract certain metals, there are attraction and repulsion forces between the poles of magnets. Like poles repel each other, whereas unlike poles attract each other.

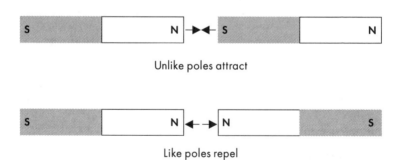

Unlike poles attract

Like poles repel

Bringing together iron and an existing magnet can make a new temporary magnet. By stroking the iron with the magnet, it is possible to line up the domains and effectively magnetise the iron. Using steel instead of iron would have a longer lasting effect.

Magnets can also be created using an electric current. If insulated copper wire is wound around an iron nail and a current passed through it an electromagnetic field is produced. This occurs because all electric currents produce a magnetic field. When the current is interrupted then the effects of the electromagnetic field are also interrupted. This means that electromagnets produce a very controllable magnetic field which can be turned on and off and also increased or decreased in strength as the current is changed. Electromagnets are used in handling scrap metal, in doorbells and loudspeakers. See **electromagnetism**.

Magnets in general have very many uses and their effects, depending on the strength of the magnet, can be felt without materials coming into contact with the magnet making them non-contact forces. Magnetic materials have uses that include recording data on magnetic tape, such as audiotapes, videotapes and computer disks, and are also very important to the operation of burglar alarms.

Magnets are also important features in electric motors where use is made of the fact that a current in a wire produces a magnetic field. In a simple motor, a current passes through a coil of wire that is located between the north and south poles of a permanent magnet. The magnetic fields of the magnet and the coil interact forcing the coil to move. To maintain this movement (using the principle of like poles repelling and unlike poles attracting), the current is reversed every half turn by a commutator. The effect is the continuous movement of the coil within the magnet.

Mass and weight

The difference between mass and weight is often confused. The mass of an object is the amount of matter in that object and remains constant. Mass is measured is kilograms (kg). The weight of an object is the effect that the force of gravity is having on that object and is measured in newtons (N). On Earth, a mass of 1 kg has a weight of 10 N. So a person with a mass of 60 kg would have a weight of 600 N. The weight of the same object on the moon is much less however. Whilst its mass will remain the same, the gravitational effect of the Moon is about one sixth that of the Earth, since it is smaller in size than Earth, so the weight of that same object is less. So, the person with a mass of 60 kg here on Earth would still have a mass of 60 kg on the Moon but their weight would be about 100 N.

Materials

When we talk about materials, we are referring to all matter, whether it is on Earth or somewhere else in the Universe. Materials can be natural (like rock, water or air) or man-made (like plastic or glass). Man-made materials tend not to occur naturally, however; they are usually made from a combination of natural materials.

All materials can be classified into groups. Some materials can be classified quite easily as being either a **solid**, a **liquid** or a **gas**. Others are a little harder. Toothpaste for example is neither completely solid, nor is it a liquid. It is also possible to sort materials according to their properties, such as:

- **absorbency**: how easily it will absorb or repel water or other liquids;
- **conductivity**: the ability to conduct heat or electrical energy. Metals are generally good conductors of both;
- **density**: the mass of a material per unit of volume;
- **elasticity**: how easily it springs back after being stretched or compressed;
- **flexibility**: how easily it will bend;
- **hardness**: how easily it can be shaped;
- **flammability**: how easily it is to ignite;
- **malleability**: how easily it can be shaped and moulded;
- **strength**: how much force is needed to break the material;
- **transparency**: how much light it allows to pass through.

Using these categories it is possible to classify most materials into one of five groups.

Material classification	Example materials	Properties
Metal	Iron, steel, copper	Hard, strong, dense, good conductors, malleable
Plastic	Polythene, PVC	Flexible, poor conductors, can be transparent, can be inflammable, low density
Ceramic	Bricks, tiles, china	Hard, brittle, medium density, rigid, may conduct heat
Glass	Bottles	Hard, brittle, medium density, rigid, may conduct heat, transparent
Fibre	Wool, cotton, paper, wood	Flexible, low density, may be flammable

Medicines

The **human body** is made from many different chemicals all working in their own individual way for the maintenance of that body. Sometimes things go wrong and the body suffers an illness. Many of these illnesses can be treated using medicines, chemicals that are taken to counter the effects of the illness. Medicines are drugs that are given in a careful and prescribed way so that the body receives sufficient for fighting the illness. They do this by interacting with the cells within the body that are causing the illness. All cells have receptors on their surface that allows them to receive messages that chemicals in the body send to the cells, often in response to fighting an illness as part of the body's immune system. Some drugs work by helping the body's chemicals and reinforcing the message they are sending to the cell. Others work by actually blocking the receptors and preventing the chemical messages being sent to the cell.

Bacteria and **viruses** can each cause illness and disease. Drugs called antibiotics can kill bacteria, which are tiny organisms. Antibiotics work by either preventing the bacteria from making a cell wall or by interfering with the way the bacteria is chemically active. Viral infections are much harder to treat using drugs because viruses inhabit body cells, and it is difficult to make a drug that will kill the virus without harming the person. Antiviral drugs block the chemicals that the virus needs to reproduce.

Melting and melting point

Every substance has a point at which, when its **temperature** is raised, it changes from a solid into a liquid. In a solid, the particles are tightly packed together and have bonds that only allow vibration about a fixed point. When a material is heated, the particles begin to vibrate much more until they reach a point where the particles are able to break free from their fixed positions and move more freely. The solid material has reached its melting point and has changed from a solid to a liquid. Different materials do this at different temperatures. The melting point of ice (made from freshwater) is 0°C, salt water has a melting point of −9°C whereas rock melts at about 600°C.

With some materials, such as paper and wood, raising the temperature will not cause change from a solid to a liquid; instead it will cause **burning** to occur.

Metallic bonding

In the **atoms** that make up a metal, the electrons in the outer shell are not attached very strongly. In fact, they are quite loose and float around in a 'sea' of electrons. These electrons flow randomly from atom to atom and the process is called metallic bonding. The flow of this sea of electrons helps to explain why metals conduct heat and electricity so well and why they have other useful characteristics such as their ability to be bent and hold a new shape.

Micro-organisms

Micro-organisms are living things that are too small to be seen without the use of a microscope. An amoeba, for example, is the size of a pinhead. Micro-organisms include bacteria, fungi, protists (single-celled organisms) and viruses. Some of these are useful to humans but others are harmful and can cause disease and illness.

- **Bacteria** are the most widespread living thing on the Earth and can be found in the air, in the ground and all over plants and animals. Some bacteria are harmful and can cause diseases; others are beneficial and are used to break down waste. A bacterium is about 1000 times smaller than an animal cell and has a thick cell wall but no nucleus. They survive either by getting their energy from chemicals or the Sun, or by the absorbtion of food from dead matter (in the decaying process). Bacteria can reproduce very quickly. In the right circumstances (warm, moist and a food supply), they can divide into two every twenty minutes or so. This means that in a period of 24 hours, some 5000 billion offspring are produced.

- *Fungi* are one of the five kingdoms of living things. Some, like yeast, are single-celled. Fungi are unable to make food of their own; instead they absorb chemicals that have been produced by other living things. These living things can be either alive or dead. If they are dead, the fungi help in the processes of decay and decomposition, breaking down the remains of plants and animals and feeding from them. Some fungi grow on living plants and animals and, in this case, can be the cause of illness and disease. Mushrooms and toadstools are just one group of a fungus, with many being edible.

- **Protists**, while being bigger than bacteria, are single celled organisms that are still too small to be seen with the naked eye. A protist cell contains a nucleus and specialised structures called organelles; these fulfil specific functions to keep the cell alive. Protists can feed in one of two ways, although some can do both:
  – by making food like plants, using the energy from the Sun;
  – by catching and eating prey.

- **Viruses** are tiny packages of chemicals that break into the cells of plants and animals. Once there, they take over the cell and prevent its normal functions taking place. Instead, the cell makes copies of the virus, dies and bursts open releasing the new viruses to continue dividing in other healthy cells. Viruses cause many illnesses such as the common cold, chicken pox, mumps, measles and HIV (Human Immunodeficiency Virus) which leads to AIDS (Acquired Immune Deficiency Syndrome). HIV effectively stops the body's natural defences from being effective leading to the attack on the body by other viruses and bacteria. In the case of most viruses, other than AIDS/HIV, the body is able to protect itself through its immune system. This is aided by immunisation, when dead viruses are injected into our bodies. This triggers a response from the immune system that produces antibodies, which attach themselves to the virus, and destroy it. Such antibodies remain in the body and continue to attack an infiltration by the same live virus.

Minerals

Minerals are substances that occur naturally in the Earth and are solids of chemical composition generally found aggregated in rocks. Rock therefore is made out of tiny crystals of minerals, each having its own chemical composition. This composition, together with fractures and weathering, contributes to determining the hardness of the rock since minerals can be classified by their hardness. A mineral that can be scratched by another mineral must be softer. A German minerologist, Friedrich Mohs, created a scale of hardness ranging from 1 to 10:

1. Talc
2. Gypsum
3. Calcite
4. Fluorite
5. Apatite
6. Orthoclase
7. Quartz
8. Topaz

9. Corundum
10. Diamond

In some rocks, the mineral can be seen easily but in others the mineral is much more difficult to spot. Some minerals are of great beauty and are used to make jewellery; others contain metals that can be removed quite easily.

Mixtures

Mixtures occur when **elements** or **compounds** are mixed together without any chemical reaction taking place. Mixtures of substances can usually be separated physically (sieving, filtering, evaporating, magnetism) whereas in a chemical compound they cannot. Solids, liquids and gases can all be mixed in different combinations and the properties of mixtures make them an aggregate of the properties of the elements in the mixture. On the other hand, a compound has its own individual properties. Different metals are often mixed together to produce alloys. The metals are heated to produce a liquid or molten metal before the two are combined into one. For example, brass is an alloy of copper and zinc.

Molecules

A molecule is a small group of two or more **atoms** that make up a **substance**. It is the smallest portion that the substance can be reduced to without losing its chemical identity. Atoms of different elements combine to form compounds, the larger particles of which are called molecules. For example, a molecule of water contains a compound of two hydrogen atoms and one atom of oxygen, hence it is symbolised by H_2O.

Moon

The Moon is a ball of rock that orbits the Earth and is the Earth's only natural satellite. It is 3456 km in diameter and orbits the Earth at a distance of 382 400 km. A complete orbit takes 27 days and 7 hours, during which time the Moon itself also rotates once on its own axis. This means that we always see the same side of the Moon from here on Earth.

Because the Earth is also in orbit around the Sun during this time, the actual length of a lunar month, the complete cycle of lunar phases, takes 29 days and 12 hours. These lunar phases are the different stages that we see of the Moon. In reality, we are looking at an increasing and decreasing amount of the daylight side of the Moon, since, like the Earth, the Moon has periods of daylight and darkness with half of the Moon in darkness and half in daylight. It is the Moon's position in relation to the Sun as it orbits around the Earth that allows us to experience the phases of the Moon. When there is a new Moon, we see the dark (night) side of the Moon. As its position changes, we begin to see a crescent as gradually we see more and more of the daylight side of the Moon.

The Moon, up to the time of a full Moon, is called a waxing Moon. After the full Moon, it is said to be waning, as slowly we see less and less until again we can only see the half of the Moon that is in darkness.

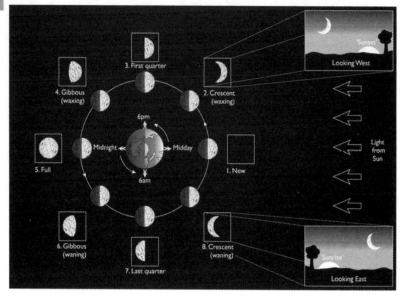

Movement

Animals, including humans, move in a variety of different ways depending on the physical characteristics of the species. All animal movement can be classified as being either voluntary or involuntary. Voluntary movement occurs when an animal moves from one place to another (locomotion) or any other action that is the result of an impulse from the animal's brain. Involuntary movement occurs when no conscious decision is taken, for example when the heart beats or we respond to pain or the eyelid blinks. These movements happen almost automatically (although we can also consciously blink our eyes).

In **plants**, most movement takes place in response to external stimuli. Plants respond to things like light and water and movement occurs, for example, as the plant grows. Most of this is observable only over a period of time (e.g. during a day). When plants react to light in this way, they are said to be phototropic. When their roots grow towards water, the plant is then said to be hydrotropic whereas when a plant grows in relation to gravity, it is said to be geotropic. Plants themselves are unable to move about since they are rooted to the ground and are therefore incapable, unlike animals, of any locomotion.

Muscle and the muscular system

The muscular system of an animal is designed to allow movement to take place. Without muscles, the animal would be unable to move about in response to stimuli received through its nervous system. Most muscles work in pairs since individual muscles are only able work in one direction: they can pull but they cannot push. Working in pairs, the muscles in the human body are arranged so that they pull in opposite directions. In the upper arm, for example, there are two main muscles that allow the arm to be bent, the biceps and the triceps. When you bend your arm at the elbow, the biceps contract and the triceps relax. When the arm is lowered, the opposite happens: the biceps relax and the triceps contract.

Animals that are **vertebrates** have three types of muscle:

1. *Voluntary or skeletal muscles*. The human has about 660 voluntary muscles that allow us to move parts of our bodies when we want to. They are fixed to our **skeletal system** using a series of tendons and have a blood supply that provides them with oxygen and glucose. Voluntary muscles are made from bundles of fibres, each fibre being a single cell. The cells in these muscles are a little different to ordinary cells in that they have many nuclei and can be more than 1 cm in length.

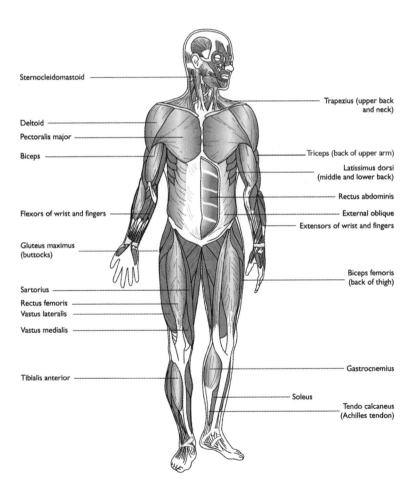

Sternocleidomastoid

Trapezius (upper back and neck)

Deltoid

Pectoralis major

Biceps

Triceps (back of upper arm)

Latissimus dorsi (middle and lower back)

Rectus abdominis

Flexors of wrist and fingers

External oblique

Extensors of wrist and fingers

Gluteus maximus (buttocks)

Biceps femoris (back of thigh)

Sartorius

Rectus femoris

Vastus lateralis

Vastus medialis

Gastrocnemius

Tibialis anterior

Soleus

Tendo calcaneus (Achilles tendon)

2. *Involuntary or smooth muscles*. These muscles are made from layers of long muscle cells and are to be found in places such as the digestive system pushing food along to aid **digestion**.

3. *Cardiac or heart muscles*. Made from branching fibres such muscles work automatically to pump blood around the body. Because they need to function continually cardiac muscles never get tired, unlike voluntary or skeletal muscles.

Mutation

Sometimes, during the biological process of copying **DNA**, mistakes happen. These mistakes, called mutations, can be caused by mutagens (a substance that causes genetic mutation), including radiation, chemicals or simply chance. Mutagens can be found in some drugs, cigarette smoke and some fumes.

Nervous system

The nervous system coordinates almost everything that the human body does. Using the senses to receive information, the nervous system is able to initiate a response to any stimuli. It is the nervous system that is the means of receiving, analysing and responding to these stimuli. The human nervous system actually consists of the central nervous system (which is the brain and spinal cord) and the peripheral nervous system (that connects the central nervous system with the rest of the body). Some of the responses the nervous system makes are under our control; others are automatic and ensure that the other body systems continue to run well.

The nervous system contains nerves; these are bundles of long, thin cells called neurons that carry electrical signals to and from the brain. There are three types of neuron:

1. *Sensory neurons* carry signals from the body to the brain or spinal cord.
2. *Motor neurons* carry signals from the brain or spinal cord to the muscles.
3. *Association neurons* carry messages between sensory neurons and motor neurons.

Neutrons

Neutrons are particles that, together with **protons**, form the nucleus of an **atom**. They are electrically neutral, carrying no charge at all, and have the same mass as a proton.

Newtons

A newton is a measure of **force** and is named after Sir Isaac Newton. He formulated the three laws of motion and explained **gravity**. A newton is described as the force which gives a **mass** of 1 kg the **acceleration** of $1 \, m/s^2$.

A newton is just one example of the **SI units** of measurements.

See also **mass and weight**.

Nuclear energy

The particles in an atom are held together by very strong bonds. This means that an atom contains a very large amount of energy. Breaking these bonds releases the energy. The **Sun** is an example of a naturally occurring nuclear reaction that produces huge amounts of energy.

On **Earth**, energy can be harnessed from the atoms of materials, such as uranium, deuterium (a type of hydrogen) and plutonium. One kilogram of deuterium can produce as much **energy** as three million kilograms of coal. It can be released through one of two processes:

1. nuclear fission where the nucleus of the atom is split;
2. nuclear fusion where the nuclei of two or more atoms are joined together.

Nuclear fission is used to release the energy that is used in the generation of **electricity** in a nuclear power station. Within a nuclear reactor, fission takes place, heat energy is produced which is then used to heat water, producing water vapour which is used to turn turbines which in turn are linked to electricity generators.

Nuclear fusion occurs in the Sun as hydrogen nuclei fuse to form helium nuclei. As yet, fusion is not a practical way of obtaining energy due to the extremely high temperatures that are required for fusion to take place.

Nutrition

All **living things** need to feed in order to grow, maintain themselves and to reproduce. In short, they need nutrients. The processes by which plants and animals receive these nutrients, or raw materials, is called nutrition. In humans, as with all animals, nutrition involves eating food, a process that is called heterotrophic nutrition. The food is then broken down through a series of physical and chemical processes so as to be absorbed and used by the body.

Food contains seven kinds of nutrients. Proteins, fats and carbohydrates are the most important although smaller quantities of minerals, vitamins, fibre and water are also needed to maintain health. The main components of food are listed in the table below.

Proteins	Proteins are essential for the growth and repair of the body. Muscles, skin, hair and nails are nearly 100% protein whereas bone is only part protein. Foods such as meat, cheese, eggs and fish provide animals with protein.
Fats and oils	Fats and oils are essential for the release and storage of energy and as a form of insulation in animals. Foods such as dairy products and fatty meats provide fats and oils.

Carbohydrates	Carbohydrates are essential for the release and storage of energy and as roughage. Foods such as bread, pasta, potatoes and rice are providers of carbohydrates.
Minerals	Minerals are vital for the building of strong bones and teeth and for the efficient functioning of the nervous system.
Vitamins	Vitamins are required in small amounts for good health. Fruit and vegetables are good sources of vitamins.
Fibre	Fibre helps to keep the digestive system clean and healthy and can be obtained from vegetables.
Water	Water is needed to carry materials around the body.

Plants feed in a different way. They make their own food, a process called autotrophic nutrition. Plants only need simple nutrients, such as carbon dioxide, water and minerals. The food that plants produce for themselves is the result of a process called **photosynthesis**. During photosynthesis, energy from the Sun combines hydrogen (from the water taken up through the plant's roots) with carbon dioxide (taken in from the atmosphere). This produces glucose and oxygen. The glucose can be used immediately to produce energy for the plant to live or stored as starch in the plant leaves.

Orbit

An orbit is the curved path or course that the planets in the **Solar System** take as they travel around the **Sun**. Each of the planets travels in its own orbit and, although they all travel in the same direction, they are travelling at different speeds and take different lengths of time to complete their orbits. The force of **gravity** is responsible for maintaining the planets in their orbit around the Sun. Its effect decreases with distance so that planets farther from the Sun travel at slower speeds.

The term orbit is also used to describe:

- the journey of the satellites of the planets, for example the **Moon** as it travels around the **Earth;**
- the journey of space rockets and telecommunication satellites as they travel around the Earth;
- the journey of asteroids and comets;
- anything that moves around something else (for example, electrons in atoms).

Organisms

Biologically an organism is described as anything that is alive. From single-celled bacteria to the largest animal or plant, all can be described as organisms. All these organisms exhibit the characteristics of living things and carry out a number of **life processes** that identify them as being alive. Because there are so many different types or **species** of organism, a system of **classification** has been developed to aid their study, recording and identification.

Particles and particulate theory

All matter is made up from many very small particles called **atoms**. These particles are so small that it would take millions to cover a full stop. Each of these particles move although the extent to which they move depends on the amount of energy they possess. It is this movement (and therefore the energy possessed and its movement) that explains how matter and materials can be either solids, liquids or gases, and how, with changes in energy levels, materials can change between the **states of matter.**

Permeability

Permeability is the ability of a **material** to allow a substance to pass through it and is therefore a characteristic of that material. For example, a material that will allow water to pass through would have a high level of permeability; others that have low levels are described as being impervious (they do not allow the substance passage). **Rocks** are often described in relation to their permeability.

Photosynthesis

Unlike animals, plants are unable to capture or gather their food, they have to make it themselves. They do this during the process of photosynthesis, which means 'putting together by light'. Plants collect energy from the Sun and use it to turn water and carbon dioxide into a simple sugar called glucose. This is then used to fuel the plant's cells and to make starch and cellulose. This all takes place not just within the leaf structure of plants, but in all green plant tissue cells. Within these tissues, there are small particles called chloroplasts which contain pigments, including the green pigment chlorophyll. When light falls on these, they trap and absorb the energy. A series of complex chemical reactions then take place during which water molecules are split apart into hydrogen and oxygen atoms. The hydrogen atoms combine with carbon dioxide to make glucose and oxygen is given off as a waste product. We cannot normally see this release of oxygen, but plants whose natural habitat is in water sometimes form bubbles on their leaves during the process of photosynthesis. Some of the water taken in by plants though their root system is used in the process of photosynthesis but most of it evaporates through the leaves, escaping together with gases through small holes called stomata.

Carbon dioxide + Water + Light energy → Glucose + Oxygen

Physical changes

Physical changes are those changes to materials that alter the appearance or other physical properties of a material or object. However, the actual substance within the material or object remains fundamentally the same.

Changes in the **state of matter** — melting, freezing, boiling, condensing and evaporating — are all examples of physical changes. When water changes and becomes a solid, a liquid or a gas, a physical change has occurred. However, since there are no chemical reactions involved, no new substance is formed and the changes that take place are reversible. This is true of most physical changes.

Physical changes are often regarded as being a change caused by:

- a change in temperature (heating or cooling) (see **evaporation, condensation, freezing, melting**);

- the application of a force in changing the shape of an object (see **forces**);

- mixing materials or substances together (see **mixtures** and **compounds**).

Plants

All living things can be divided into one of five major groups or kingdoms. The plant kingdom is just one of these groups and in general can be thought of as consisting of a number of smaller divisions or phyla (sing. phylum).

Kingdom: Plants	
Phylum	
Club mosses	400 species
Conifers	550 species
Ferns	12 000 species
Horsetails	550 species
Mosses and liverworts	25 000 species
Flowering plants **Subphylum:** Monocotyledons Dicotyledons	250 000 species Irises, grasses and orchids Elms, legumes, daisies, roses, cacti, foxgloves, parsley and carrots, cabbages, oaks and heathers

Non–flowering plants first appeared some 300 million years ago and include conifers, ferns and mosses. They reproduce by shedding and spreading spores. Conifers, however, while they are non–flowering do not grow from spores. Instead they produce cones, which make either male or female cells. These are carried from male to female where the seeds are then produced.

Flowering plants spread pollen from flower to flower in order to fertilise the female sex cells and produce seeds. Flowering plants have a number of different ways of **seed dispersal** to ensure that new plants do not compete with their parents for valuable resources.

Plants carry out the **life processes** associated with living things and make their own food through the process of **photosynthesis**. The structure of flowering plants is generally a shared characteristic although clearly there are variations within and between **species**.

Structure of Flowering Plants	
Roots	Roots are very important to the health and well-being of any plant and perform two major functions. 1. Roots supply water to a plant. Plants need water to survive. If a plant becomes short of water it will wilt and eventually die. The roots, many with tiny hairs, draw up water and trace minerals from the ground which are transported to the leaves where **photosynthesis** takes place. Some water is lost as it evaporates from the leaves and flower, a process called transpiration. The water in the roots (and stem) moves due to a combination of capillary attraction (very narrow tubular structures pull liquids upwards) and evaporation from the leaves which pulls water up through the roots and stem. 2. The root system acts as an anchor and holds the plant firmly in place. Without a well-established root system, the plant would rock about in the wind, become very loose, fall over and die. The root system of some plants is very extensive and those of trees can cause structural damage to nearby buildings. 3. Roots supply some essential nutrients from the soil to aid plant growth and health. In certain soil conditions, roots cannot obtain these nutrients and this function is taken over by the flower (insectivorous plants). Not all plants are rooted in the ground. Some plants have aerial roots while others may be rooted onto other plants.
Stems	Stems have two functions in maintaining healthy plants: 1. It is the stem or stems of a plant that hold it upright and in a position to most benefit from its environmental circumstances. This includes holding flowers and leaves so that they can benefit from the light from the Sun. 2. Stems are also part of the transport system within a plant. The stem consists of tiny tubes called xylem along which the fluids travel and phloem which lead from the leaves to the stem and are the means of transporting food around the plant.
Leaves	The main function of leaves is the production of food during the process of **photosynthesis**. The upper side of a leaf has a layer of cells called palisade cells, which contain chloroplasts (as do all green tissue **cells**), while the underside has small air holes called stomata that are used for **respiration** and **excretion**.
Flowers	The flower is the part of the plant that is responsible for reproduction; it is here that seeds are formed. Flowers generally consist of: The reproductive part: • *male*: the stamen consisting of the anther (a small sac where pollen grains are made) and the filament (a stalk); • *female*: the ovary (a hollow where the seeds begin to form) that may consist of one or more carpels and a stigma (an area where the pollen is received), which in many flowers is held on a stalk, called a style. Other parts: • *nectary*: the place where nectar for insects is sometimes produced; • *petals*: that are usually brightly coloured to attract insects; • *sepals*: a green outer ring that protects the flower when it is still a bud; • *receptacle*: an area that supports the flower located at the end of the plant stalk or stem; In some plants, the flower obtains essential nutrients, such as nitrogen, by -attracting or drowning insects (e.g. pitcher plants).

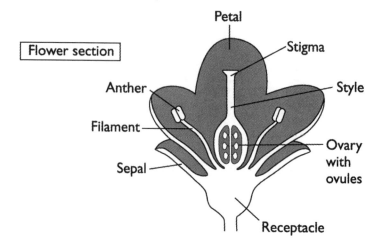

Petal

Flower section

Stigma

Anther

Style

Filament

Ovary
with
ovules

Sepal

Receptacle

Pollination

The flower is the part of a plant that is responsible for the production of seeds through sexual reproduction. Pollination is the first part of this process. It occurs when a pollen grain lands on the flower's stigma (female sex organ) and can come from the same flower when self–pollination occurs, or from another flower, a process called cross–pollination.

Living things often act as pollinators as they carry pollen from flower to flower. Insects, which are not the only pollinators, are attracted to plants by the scent and colour of their flowers and in so doing transfer pollen. Eager to feed on the nectar the flower may have produced, the insect unwittingly collects on its body grains of pollen. These are then transferred from the body of the insect onto the stigma of another flower by the unknowing insect.

Pollen grains can also be carried by the wind from flower to flower.

Once pollinated, the male and female sex cells join up during **fertilisation**.

Pollution

Pollution can be described as damage caused to the environment and can take many different forms and have serious consequences. As humans, we pollute the Earth in a number of ways with differing consequences:

- Air pollution caused by the discharge into the atmosphere of waste materials, smoke, gases and exhaust fumes can cause damage to the health of both plants and animals. Such waste gases could have been a contributory factor in an increase in the temperature of the Earth known as 'global warming'.

Carbon dioxide, which is produced when fossil fuels are burnt, has molecules that are heavier than those of oxygen and nitrogen so heat radiation does not pass through them as easily. This means that heat from the Earth is trapped and the result is a warming in the climate of the Earth. This can affect many regions of the Earth and consequences include reduced rainfall levels that result in changes to crop growth and the increased chance of flooding as areas of the polar ice caps melt. The possibility of raised sea levels is also increased.

Gases used in some products often referred to as CFCs, or chlorofluro-carbons, are characteristically heavier than carbon dioxide and have a very similar effect on the environment.

These so called 'greenhouse' gases could be responsible for damage caused to the ozone layer (a part of the Earth's **atmosphere**), which has resulted in more of the Sun's ultraviolet radiation being able to reach the Earth, again causing 'global warming'. This extra ultraviolet radiation can also cause damage to plants and could increase (together with other factors) the risk of humans developing skin cancers.

- Waste materials being dumped on the land, in rivers and in the sea can cause environmental damage since many such materials are not biodegradable (they cannot be decomposed by organisms such as **bacteria**) and so remain as they are for perhaps hundreds of years. Some waste may contain poisonous liquids that can leak out and run into watercourses, produce dangerous gases or catch fire.

- Sound pollution from traffic, domestic appliances, TV and music systems is considerably louder than in previous decades and is now thought to cause some hearing loss in children regularly exposed to continuous sound pollution.

- Light pollution in large towns and cities means that we can no longer see the night sky with any detail. Before buildings and street light became the norm, it would have been possible on a clear night to see stars, planets and the Milky Way.

- Electromagnetic radiation can be thought of as pollution when nuclear installations and man-made appliances damage our environment. Some people appear to be affected by living near pylons or telephone transmitting stations and the frequent use of mobile telephones is causing concern. Government guidelines (2002) suggest using shields over mobile telephones to reduce the levels of electromagnetic radiation near the head or body.

Potential energy
See **energy**

Producer

Green plants use light energy from the Sun in order to make food during the process of **photosynthesis**. Plants and other organisms capable of photosynthesis are therefore referred to as being autotrophs or primary producers. Other organisms obtain their energy by eating these producers and are called **consumers**.

Protons

The nucleus of all **atoms** (everything is made from tiny particles called atoms) contain two types of particles: neutrons and protons. The number of protons in an atom gives the atom its atomic number. Protons are electrically positive and together with **neutrons** and **electrons** are called subatomic particles. Protons and neutrons have virtually the same mass, almost the same as the mass of a hydrogen atom. One proton therefore is described as having a relative mass of one, like the hydrogen atom.

Reflection

We are able to see objects because **light** from a light source is reflected from that object and into our eyes. Most surfaces that reflect light scatter it so that it is reflected in different directions. These are often made from materials that have rough, dull surfaces. This allows us to see objects when we move into different positions. Some materials do not behave like this. Instead, they reflect light directly and often in a regular and somewhat predictable way. Smooth and shiny surfaces such as mirrors are good examples of this. When light is reflected from a flat mirror, it is reflected from the mirror at the same angle as it hits it.

When you look at a reflection in a flat or plane mirror, you see what is called a virtual image. It is so called because neither the object or the image are where they appear to be. For example, if you stand 1 metre away from a mirror and look at your reflection, the image also appears to be 1 metre away from the mirror. What you see is a virtual image of yourself. Because the light from the mirror is reflected straight back, the image is formed exactly the same distance 'behind' the mirror as you are in front of the mirror and is the same size. The image is, however, different from the 'original' in that if you lift your left hand, the image moves its right, something that is called lateral inversion.

Curved mirrors also reflect light and produce images but the curve of the mirror affects the image as it allows light to be reflected not straight back but either concentrated or spread out. Concave mirrors, those that curve inwards, concentrate the light rays and give a strong parallel beam of light from its surface. Concave mirrors are often used in torches and spotlights.

Convex mirrors, on the other hand, spread out the rays of light and give a much wider field of view. These are used as driving and shaving mirrors since the image is of a much larger size than that in a plane mirror.

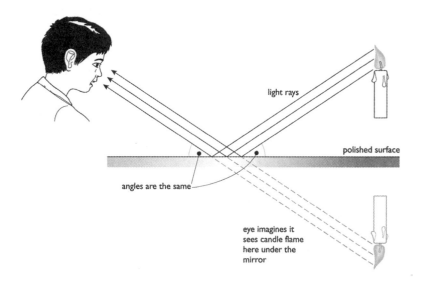

light rays

polished surface

angles are the same

eye imagines it
sees candle flame
here under the
mirror

Refraction

When **light** travelling through the air meets a transparent material such as glass or water, the light changes direction away from a straight-line path. This is known as refraction and is caused by the slowing of the light as it passes through different materials. For example, when light passes through a prism, it is refracted because of the glass, and where the light meets the prism at an angle, light is diffracted into its constituent colours (see **colour**). Refraction also often gives rise to some unusual and unexpected effects. When light passes from air into water, refraction occurs and makes the water appear to be shallower than it really is. Similarly, when a pencil is stood ob-liquely in a glass of water, it appears to be bent and the stick appears in a position that in reality it is not. This can also be observed when trying to locate something at the bottom of a bath full of water!

Renewable energy

Energy comes in many different forms and from different fuel sources. Many of these fuel sources, such as the **fossil fuels** (coal, oil, gas) will eventually run out. They are non-renewable which means that once used they are gone forever. Alternatively, renewable fuels are those than will not run out in the foreseeable future. They are replaceable and include:

- **Water power.** In a hydroelectric power station, the kinetic energy of falling water is used to drive turbines that in turn drive a generator that produces electrical energy. Hydroelectric power systems are able to generate electricity at very short notice since they do not involve the lighting up of furnaces to produce heat — they simply require a flow of water.

- **Tidal power.** Very similar to more conventional hydroelectric power schemes but the flow of water comes from the rise and fall of the tides. As the tide comes in, water is stored behind a barrage to be released when the tide is out and to again turn a system of turbines and generators.

- **Solar power.** The Sun's energy can be converted into electrical energy inside photovoltaic or solar cells similar to those found in solar powered calculators. The Sun will eventually 'expire' but not in the foreseeable future.

- **Wind power.** Modern day windmills are used as wind turbines to generate electricity. Wind power generation, however, is susceptible to changes in the patterns of wind experienced in any particular place.

Reproduction and the reproductive system

All living things share one basic feature in life: reproduction. It is this motivation to reproduce that ensures the continuation of the species. This reproduction can occur in one of two ways:

1. asexual reproduction;
2. sexual reproduction.

Asexual reproduction involves just one parent and does not involve sex. Part of the parent breaks or splits away and grows and develops into a new individual living thing. The process is quick and simple but does, however, have the drawback of both the parent and offspring sharing the same genetic material. Any genetic defects are therefore passed on and are not naturally bred out of the species. This means that the power to adapt is reduced and natural selection takes over.

Most asexual reproduction takes place in plants although some animals such as the hydra (a tiny animal living in ponds) also reproduce asexually. The sea anemone is one animal that can reproduce asexually as well as sexually, so too is the aphid.

Plants can reproduce or be reproduced asexually in a number of ways:

- **By sending out runners.** Plants such as the strawberry send out horizontal stems which develop young plants at the end and send down roots into the soil. The stems then die back and the new plant becomes independent of its parent.

- **By producing bulbs.** As plants such as the daffodil and garlic grow and develop, new small bulbs are produced around its base. These themselves will grow and develop into independent plants. This explains why, if left in the ground, a few daffodil bulbs will develop over the years into a large number of plants.

- *Through their roots*. Some plants are able to reproduce from the remains of roots left in the ground. Gardeners know only too well how important it is to take out all the root system of a 'weed' to prevent it from reproducing new plants from all the pieces of root that are left.

We also make use of asexual reproduction as farmers and gardeners, and assist in the reproduction of plants by taking cuttings from the leaves and stems of certain plants and growing them on. It is possible to grow cuttings from one plant by grafting them onto another, related plant (e.g. fruit trees). This does not always produce a new species: in time, the graft usually returns to the original stock.

The process of sexual reproduction requires there to be two parents. Each parent is responsible for the production of sex cells or gametes. These cells, the male sperm and the female egg, are combined during fertilisation and a new cell is formed from which the new plant or animal develops. Sexual reproduction takes longer than asexual reproduction but has the advantage that, rather than being genetically identical to the parent, the offspring inherit half of their **genes** from one of their parents and half from the other. This means that any genetic weaknesses may not always be carried on from one generation to another, although this does happen in some circumstances where the gene carrying a particular characteristic is dominant.

Sexual reproduction can take place in one of two ways:

- *External reproduction*. Some animals are able reproduce in a way that requires no sexual union. Eggs laid by the female are fertilised outside the body by the male's sperm. Animals that reproduce in this way tend to lay large numbers of eggs to increase the chances of fertilisation and survival of the offspring.

- *Internal reproduction*. In some animal species, internal reproduction involves the sexual union or mating of the male and female. The male injects his sperm into the female so that fertilisation can take place inside the female's body. In mammals, the female then carries the young as it grows and develops from two cells to millions. This period is called the gestation period and its length varies from one species to another. Others species, like birds, lay fertilised eggs that are incubated until the young bird hatches. Animals that reproduce in this way tend to produce fewer sex cells as there is more likelihood of successful fertilisation taking place.

Human reproduction takes place through internal sexual fertilisation. During sexual intercourse sperm, produced in the male's testes, is mixed with a liquid in the prostate gland to produce semen. This then travels through the penis and enters the vagina of the female. Here, sperm swim into the uterus and along the fallopian tubes. If the female has ovulated (produced a ripe egg cell), the sperm may fertilise the egg and a zygote is formed. Only one sperm is required for fertilisation to occur out of the millions that are ejaculated from the male. Once fertilised, the zygote begins to change as it divides and develops. If this division leads to each part developing into a baby, then each will have the same genes, both will be either male or female and will be identical twins. If two eggs (or more) are released from the ovary and are fertilised, they will have different genes, may be either male or female and will be non–identical twins (or triplets etc).

The fertilised egg then travels down the fallopian tube to the uterus where it implants in the lining of the womb and where the placenta also develops. The zygote continues to grow into an embryo (in humans the first eight weeks after conception), and then a foetus (an unborn offspring over eight weeks since conception).

During the next nine months, the embryo is provided with food and oxygen through the umbilical cord, along which waste materials from the baby are also passed. As the embryo becomes fully developed, the female gives birth (usually after 40 weeks) with the baby being born through the female's vagina.

Whereas asexual reproduction is widespread in plants and sexual reproduction widespread in animals, there are many plants (such as the strawberry) and some animals (such as the sea anemone) that are able reproduce both asexually and sexually.

Respiration and the respiratory process

All living things, including plants and animals, need energy to survive and carry out their functions and other **life processes**. Animals get their energy from the food they eat and plants from the food they produce as a result of **photosynthesis**. In animals, including humans, nutrients, including carbohydrates, are transported around the body in **blood** cells and then into **cells** of the body. Here, the digested food is broken down so that the **energy** it contains can be released and put to use within the body. This process is called respiration. There are two types of respiration: aerobic, which occurs when oxygen is present; and anaerobic, which occurs when there is no oxygen present.

Aerobic respiration is the process that results in glucose being oxygenated to produce carbon dioxide and water during which a great deal of energy is released. This energy is used by the body to help it function effectively. In anaerobic respiration, because of the lack of oxygen, the glucose is turned not into carbon dioxide and water but into lactic acid. Organisms, such as yeasts and bacteria, can live entirely by anaerobic respiration and can be useful to humans. For example, respiration of yeast cells results in the production of ethanol, an alcohol and carbon dioxide substance used in brewing and bread–making respectively.

Respiration also occurs in plants. As they photosynthesise, plants build up food in the form of glucose and starch. Some of this food is broken down through respiration but plants make more food than they break down so their leaves take in carbon dioxide. At night, when the photosynthesis stops, plants continue to break down food by respiration but now their leaves need to take in oxygen due to the absence of light.

$$\text{Glucose} + \text{Oxygen} \rightarrow \text{Carbon dioxide} + \text{Water} + \text{Energy}$$

Rocks

The surface of the **Earth**, the Earth's crust, is made up from layers of rock, though much of it is in turn covered by layers of soil or by water. Rock is classified according to the way in which it was formed many millions of years ago. Rocks are still forming today and some carbonates (a salt of carbonic acid) actually form within a matter of hours.

Three types of rock make up the Earth's crust.

1. *Igneous rock* is rock that is formed when molten rock cools, hardens and becomes a solid. There are two types of igneous rock (also called 'rocks of fire'): extrusive and intrusive. Extrusive igneous rock, such as basalt, is formed from the lava flow of a volcano. When the lava reaches the surface of the Earth, it cools fairly quickly and produces a fine-grained rock. Granite, on the other hand, is an example of an intrusive igneous rock, that is one that cools and solidifies not on the surface of the Earth but underground. Granite forms when magma cools very slowly and produces a coarse grained rock. Igneous rock is generally very hard and is often used on road surfaces.

2. *Metamorphic rocks* are rocks that have been changed into harder rocks by enormous pressure or high temperatures. These rocks undergo a structural change in their mineral composition and texture and are therefore called metamorphic rocks. Both sedimentary rocks and igneous rocks are subject to the pressure and heat that can be found deep under the surface of the Earth and can both become metamorphic rocks. Typical examples of metamorphic rocks are slate, which is formed under intense pressure from shale, and some marble, which is formed when limestone comes into contact with hot igneous rock.

3. *Sedimentary rocks* are formed during a build-up of layers of particles that are then compressed and cemented together by further layers of particles. These particles of sediment are often the result of weathering and so may be formed from other rock types or may be the remains of plant and animal life. As the layers of sediment build up over many millions of years, the compression forms soft rocks such as coal, sandstone and chalk. Layers that are buried deeper are compressed further and become much harder rocks such as limestone. Sedimentary rocks are used in a variety of ways, the harder ones being used as building materials.

Rocks are used for a variety of purposes largely in the construction of buildings, with many rocks having very distinctive characteristics such as their colour, strength and workability.

Rock kits containing samples of different rocks are available from Hardy Aggregates, Shepton Mallet (www.hardy-aggregates.co.uk)

Rusting

When iron and steel are exposed to moisture and air, they will begin to rust. This rust is the result of an oxidation reaction which occurs when a substance combines with oxygen. In rusting, oxygen combines with the iron to produce iron oxide while, at the same time, the moisture in the air combines with the iron to form hydrated iron oxide or rust. Once the top layer of the iron or steel has rusted, oxygen from the air reaches the inner layers causing further oxidation. The rusting of iron and steel can be prevented by:

- oiling and greasing to create a waterproof protective layer;
- painting to keep air and water away from the iron and steel;
- coating with plastic as a means of creating a protective layer;
- galvanising, where a layer of another metal is applied over the iron or steel.

Seasons

The **Earth** rotates about an axis that is inclined at an angle of 23.5° to the vertical. This causes not only variations in the length of daylight hours during the course of a year but also the seasons. Seasonal changes in the weather and the length of daylight occur because, as the Earth rotates, it also orbits the Sun, while always being inclined on exactly the same plane. This means that parts of the Earth are facing the Sun for longer periods of time. For example, the northern hemisphere is tilted towards the Sun during the summer and tilted away from the Sun in winter. This 'tilt' leads to a variation in the heating effects of the Sun on the hemispheres. During the summer, when the northern hemisphere is tilted towards the Sun, the daylight hours are longer and the amount of solar energy falling on that hemisphere is greater in terms of the length of time it falls and its concentration. In the winter, the opposite applies: the northern hemisphere is tilted away from the Sun, daylight hours are short and the solar energy received is more spread out.

In Britain, the seasons are:

Season	Begins	Characteristics
Spring	21 March	Spring equinox: day and night are of equal length
Summer	21 June	Summer solstice: daylight is at its longest
Autumn	22 September	Autumnal equinox: day and night are of equal length
Winter	21 December	Winter solstice: daylight is at its shortest

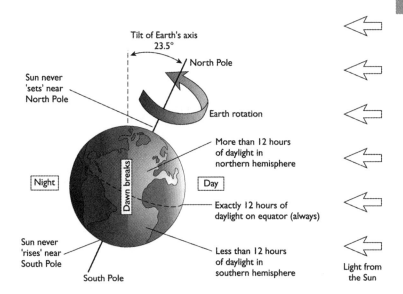

Tilt of Earth's axis
23.5°

North Pole

Sun never
'sets' near
North Pole

Earth rotation

More than 12 hours
of daylight in
northern hemisphere

Night

Dawn breaks

Day

Exactly 12 hours of
daylight on equator (always)

Sun never
'rises' near
South Pole

Less than 12 hours
of daylight in
southern hemisphere

South Pole

Light from
the Sun

The Met Office (http://www.meto.gov.uk/education/curriculum/leaf-lets/seasons.html) offer online resources for teaching and learning at Key Stages 1 and 2, including worksheets and classroom activities for teaching about the seasons.

Seed dispersal

For the continuation of the species, flowering **plants** produce seeds which need appropriate conditions in which to germinate. These conditions are often away from the parent plant so that the competition for the conditions present in that location, or for particular nutrients, is reduced. This is achieved in a number of different ways.

- *Animal dispersal.* Many seeds are contained in fruits and berries that are eaten by birds and animals. These birds and animals then move around and, as they do so, the seeds are passed out of their bodies as waste. Some seeds are contained in fruit that have cases or shells with hooks on them. These cling onto animals as they pass and are carried away from the plants to be brushed off elsewhere. Seeds contained within nuts and shells are often taken by animals for food and stored, ready to be eaten during the winter. Animals often drop these in this process or collect more than they eat. This results in those that are not eaten being able to germinate given the appropriate conditions.

- *Explosive dispersal.* Some plants have mechanisms that allow them to disperse their seeds through a tiny 'explosion'. Peas, for example, have seeds inside pods that dry out and then burst open spilling their contents away from the parent plant.

- *Fire dispersal*. Some plants have evolved to take advantage of forest fires (e.g. Australian banksia and grasses). The fire heats up the very tough seed heads which pop open and eject their seeds into the cooling, fertile ash.

- *Water dispersal*. Some plants have seeds which are dropped from the plant onto water. The seeds float and are carried along until coming to ground where they can begin to germinate.

- *Wind dispersal*. Many flowering plants, such as the dandelion, produce seeds with light feathery attachments. When the time is right, these are blown away by the wind to germinate. Some trees, such as the sycamore, have seeds which are attached to a 'helicopter' type case which, when released by the tree, float and flutter away rather than dropping directly down from the tree.

Senses and sensitivity

For a variety of reasons, including survival, both plants and animals have evolved sensory systems that inform them of their **environment** and the conditions that exist there. This sensitivity allows them to respond in an appropriate way, a response that in many instances requires some sort of change or movement, either voluntary or involuntary. In animals, this sensitivity to the environment is very well developed through the use of specialised sensory organs and a nervous system. In humans, the five senses are sight, hearing, smell, taste and touch.

Sense	Sensory organ	Stimulus
Sight	Eyes	Light
Hearing	Ears	Sound
Smell	Nose	Chemicals in the nose
Taste	Tongue	Chemicals in the mouth
Touch	Skin	Forces on the skin

When the sensory organs detect a stimulus, messages pass along nerves in the central nervous system of an animal to the brain. The brain decides if a response is required and, if it is, impulses are passed along the nerves and cause the muscles to move.

The human body, like most animals, also has a second system for responding to stimuli as well as to the nervous system. The endocrine system contains glands that produce hormones. These hormones are chemicals that are released into the blood from various glands and produce specific responses in humans.

Hormone	Gland	Effects of hormone
Adrenaline	Adrenal	Prepares the body for movement and action by speeding up the heart and breathing rates.
Growth hormone	Pituitary	Speeds up growth.
Insulin	Pancreas	Controls blood sugar levels; a deficiency is the cause of diabetes.
Oestrogen and progesterone	Ovaries	Control female sexual development, begin puberty and regulate the menstrual cycles and ovulation.
Testosterone	Testes	Controls male sexual development, begins puberty and regulates the production of sperm.
Thyroxine	Thyroid	Controls the rate that chemicals are processed in the body (metabolism) and growth.
Tropic hormones	Pituitary	Stimulates other glands into producing their own hormones.

Plants also respond to stimuli and have evolved a system that allows them to respond. The main stimuli in plants are light and gravity. A plant will tend to grow towards the light in order to maximise the plant's surface area exposed to the light, so that **photosynthesis** can take place. Responses that plants make are called tropisms. Generally, they occur quite slowly and tend to be less varied than responses in animals. This response to light is called photo-tropism and occurs because auxin (a plant hormone that controls growth) gathers at the growth tips furthest away from the light. Faster growth there-fore takes place here resulting in the plant bending towards the light. A plant's response to the stimulus of gravity is geotropism. Geotropism results in plants growing vertically, even on steep slopes and the production of shoots and roots which grow vertically upwards and downwards. Sensitivity in plants allows them to respond to the best growing conditions, to root in appropriate places, to send out roots to gather water and minerals, and to climb and grow to maximise photosynthesis and therefore growth.

Separation

Some materials that occur naturally do so mixed together with other materi-als in a mixture. Separating these materials from each other is sometimes needed to be able to use the individual materials.

Separating solid materials can be achieved by:

- *Sieving*. Solids of different sizes can be separated by passing the mix-ture through a sieve. The smaller particles fall through and the larger ones are retained in the sieve.

- *Decanting*. This is used to separate insoluble solids from liquids. The mixture is left to settle with the insoluble solid falling to the bottom of the liquid; this can then be poured off leaving the solid behind.

- *Filtering*. This is used to separate insoluble solids from liquids. The mixture is poured through fine paper with tiny holes in it — the solid is unable to pass freely through the paper unlike the liquid.

- *Centrifuging*. This is used to separate very small particles that float in a liquid forming a suspension. The suspension, if spun around very quickly, forces the denser solid particles to the end of the container allowing the liquid to be decanted away.

When a solid and liquid are mixed, a solution is formed. These can also be separated. See **solutions**.

Shadows

Shadows are formed when **light** travelling in a straight line from a light source meets an object. The object blocks the light, which is either absorbed or reflected. Shadows are produced in the area behind the object blocking the light. Shadows vary in quality and size. An object that effectively blocks the light produces a much more distinct shadow. The overall shape of a shadow corresponds to that of the object casting the shadow. For example, a child standing outside on a sunny day would cast a shadow that is indicative of their shape and size.

However, the size and position of a shadow changes as either the object changes or the light source moves. A good example of this can be seen with shadows cast by the **Sun**. In the early morning, when we see the Sun low in our sky (the Sun remains in the same place, it is the **Earth** that is moving), the shadows that are cast are very long. As the day progresses towards midday, when the Sun is at its apparent highest in the sky, the shadows become shorter and shorter. If we could stand with the Sun directly overhead at midday (e.g. at the Equator), we would not cast any shadow at all except under our feet. During the afternoon, the shadows get longer again until the evening when they are again, just like early morning, very long.

A number of factors affect the quality of a shadow. These include the relative size of the light source, the objects used to block the light, the distance of the object from the light source and the distance from the object to the surface on which the shadow is cast. Shadows can also be lightened by light that is reflected from the object's surroundings.

Shadows cast by the Sun have two parts: an umbra and a penumbra. The umbra is the area of total shadow where an object blocks all of the light from the Sun, whereas the penumbra is the area in partial shade around the edge of the shadow. Shadows cast by the Sun also create the phenomenon of an **eclipse**, both solar and lunar. Shadows were used for many years as a means of telling the time of day. The Chinese used sundials over 4000 years ago where a simple stick, now called a gnomon, was used to cast a shadow on a dial. Sundials are still used today but more generally as ornaments.

SI units

SI units are an internationally agreed system of units used for scientific and other purposes. SI means Système International d'Unités and includes among others the following symbols:

Symbol	Unit	Explanation
A	Ampere	A measure of the flow of an electrical current
J	Joule	A measure of energy
kg	Kilogram	A measure of the mass of an object
m	Metre	A measure of distance
N	Newton	A measure of force
s	Second	A measure of time
V	Volt	A measure of voltage, the push that drives a current around a circuit
W	Watt	A measure of power, the rate at which work is done or energy used
Ω	Ohm	A measure of the resistance of a component in an electrical circuit
Hz	Hertz	A measure of frequency
°C	Degree Celsius	A measure of Celsius temperature
dB	Decibel	A measure of the intensity of a sound

Skeletal system

A skeleton is a framework that supports and protects the body of some animals. In humans, this framework is made up largely from bone and cartilage. Bone helps to give strength to the framework while cartilage at the joints allows movement to take place. The human body has about 206 bones ranging from the large bones to be found in the thigh to the small bones in the inner ear.

The skeleton has a number of main functions:

- it protects important parts of the body, for example the brain is protected by the skull, the internal organs are protected by the ribs and the spinal cord is protected by the backbone;

- it gives support and shape, allowing humans to stand up and gives a framework to the body;

- it allows movement to take place using the muscles that are attached to the bones by strong fibrous tissue called tendons.

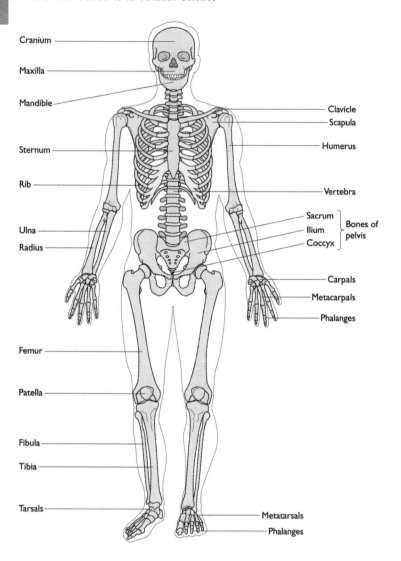

Cranium
Maxilla
Mandible
Sternum
Rib
Ulna
Radius
Femur
Patella
Fibula
Tibia
Tarsals

Clavicle
Scapula
Humerus
Vertebra
Sacrum
Ilium — Bones of pelvis
Coccyx
Carpals
Metacarpals
Phalanges
Metatarsals
Phalanges

Soil

Soil is made up from **rocks**, minerals and humus. Over millions of years, the rocks have been broken up into tiny pieces and these together with minerals and the humus (decaying plant life or organic matter) are mixed together by, among other things, climatic change to form soil. This mixture becomes a habitat for living things, such as plants and minibeasts, and just as there are different types of rock so too are there different types of soil. These different soil types are produced depending on the underlying rock types in the area and have different properties. Some rocks differ in their chemical nature and can produce acid (e.g. clay types) or alkaline soils. Some soils differ in texture. Some are fine, some are gritty and open and some are more solid with particles that stick together. Some of these different soil types are listed below.

- Sandy soil is gritty and drains water quickly. It is often low in nutrients and contains very little organic matter making it not very fertile.

- Clay soil is very heavy and does not drain very well. It holds together without crumbling and is very sticky when wet.

- Chalky soil is very stony with pieces of chalk being very evident. It is quick to drain, contains very quick decaying organic matter and so only contains small amounts of humus.

- Loamy soil holds water well and contains good levels of organic matter. Plants grow well in loamy soils.

- Peaty soil is dark coloured and contains good levels of rich organic matter. It absorbs a good amount of water and is formed in bog and fen land.

Soils are also formed in a number of different layers, called horizons. These represent the different stages of soil production.

- Horizon 0 is the humus layer where plant material is deposited prior to decaying.

- Horizon A is the topsoil. It is rich in organic matter although some minerals are washed out by water in the ground.

- Horizon B is the subsoil and contains much less organic matter. It does however contain many minerals washed down from the topsoil.

- Horizon C is the parent rock from which chunks are broken off and ground down.

- Horizon D is the underlying bedrock. The mineral content of the soil is derived from this layer of rock.

Solar system

The Solar System is the name we give to our **Sun** and the planets that orbit around it. Even though it is some 12 000 million kilometres in diameter, our Solar System is just one of millions of star systems that make up the galaxy called the Milky Way. There are billions of such galaxies, that we know about, in the **Universe**.

Asteroids (minor planets mostly located between Mars and Jupiter), comets (huge balls of ice) and moons (rocks that orbit planets) together with large quantities of interplanetary dust also form part of the Solar System.

The Sun, the centre of the Solar System, has nine planets in orbit around it which were formed 4600 million (4.6 billion) years ago, some 400 million years after the Sun was born. Each planet follows an individual orbit and travels at a different speed yet all follow in the same direction around the Sun. The planets are kept in their orbits by the force of **gravity**. Gravity is a force of attraction between any two bodies that have a **mass**. Its strength depends on the mass of each body and how far apart they are. Planets further from the Sun are less affected by the gravity of the Sun (which accounts for 99% of the mass of our Solar System) and therefore travel slower in their orbits.

	Mercury	Venus	Earth	Mars	Jupiter	Saturn	Uranus	Neptune	Pluto
Distance from the Sun in millions of km	57.9	108.2	149.6	227.9	778.3	1427	2870	4497	5913
Diameter at Equator in km	4879	12 104	12 756	6786	142 984	120 536	51 118	49 528	2284
Time to orbit the Sun	87.97 days	224.7 days	365.25 days	686.98 days	11.86 years	29.46 years	84.01 years	164.8 years	248.5 years
Time to turn 360 degrees	58.65 days	243.01 days	24 hours	24h 37m	9h 55m	10h 39m	17h 14m	16h 7m	6 days 9hrs
Atmosphere	Almost none	Clouds of sulphuric acid gas	Carbon dioxide, water vapour and nitrogen	Very thin	Contains methane, ammonia, hydrogen and helium	Ammonia and other chemicals	Hydrogen, helium and methane	Hydrogen, helium and methane	Unknown
Temperature	−200°C- to +400°C	480°C	−70°C to +55°C	−120°C to +25°C	−150°C	−180°C	−214°C	−220°C	−230°C

My **V**ery **E**asy **M**ethod **J**ust **S**hows **U N**ine **P**lanets:

- **M**ercury is the closest planet to the Sun and has a gravity of less than half that of the Earth. This makes it too weak to hold gas around the planet and so Mercury has virtually no atmosphere. With no atmosphere, sound is unable to travel so Mercury is a silent planet and while it also has the biggest difference between day and night temperatures of all the planets, it is not actually the hottest planet.

- **V**enus has an atmosphere that consists of thick clouds of sulphuric acid gas that act like a greenhouse, trapping the energy from the Sun and causing the temperature to rise to 480°C. With a surface pressure some 100 times that of the Earth, Venus is a most inhospitable planet.

- **E**arth is sometimes called the 'Blue Planet' because its atmosphere scatters the light from the Sun and creates a mainly blue effect. With two-thirds of its surface covered by water and an atmosphere of nitrogen and oxygen the Earth is able to sustain a huge range of plant and animal life. This is only possible because the size of the planet Earth is such that its gravitational force holds the atmosphere around it. It is thought that the Moon may have once had an atmosphere but its gravitational force was too small to keep it. See **gravity**.

- **M**ars is often called the 'Red Planet' because of the red dust and rock that covers its surface. It has gravity half of that on Earth and so it is only able to hold a very thin atmosphere around it. The surface of Mars is covered with deep craters, high mountains and deserts.

- **J**upiter is a giant in the Solar System in that it contains three times more mass than the other eight planets put together. It is made mostly of gases and liquids with a small rocky core. Its atmosphere is 1280 km thick and contains methane, ammonia, hydrogen and helium.

- **S**aturn is another gas giant with a mass 95 times that of the Earth. It has no real surface and its density is so low that it is the only planet lighter than the same volume of water. Placed in a big enough pool of water (if you were able to do so), Saturn would float because of this low density. Saturn is best known for its rings that are actually made out of pieces of icy rock.

- **U**ranus is four times the size of the Earth and has a blue-green ball of gas as its atmosphere. It has 15 moons and a number of faint rings around it.

- **N**eptune is another gas giant with no real surface. With wind speeds of up 2000 km/h, Neptune is one of the windiest planets in the Solar System.

- **P**luto is the smallest planet in our Solar System. It is thought to possibly have a thin atmosphere and a frost covered surface. It is nearly 40 times further from the Sun than the Earth and is a very dark planet due to its composition. The Sun probably just looks like a bright star from Pluto because of its distance.

The nine named planets are not the only objects orbiting the Sun as part of our Solar System. Asteroids, comets and meteors are all fairly significant and are very many in number. There are millions of chunks of rock ranging in size, from dust to a few hundred kilometres in diameter, called asteroids. Although not proper planets these are often regarded as being minor planets. Most, but not all of them, are in orbit between Mars and Jupiter in an area of space called the asteroid belt. Asteroids are actually pieces of material that did not form themselves into proper planets because they were prevented from clumping together due to the massive gravitational effect of nearby Jupiter.

Comets are also the leftovers of the cloud that formed our Solar System and are basically chunks of ice and rock. Often referred to as 'dirty snowballs', there are billions of comets on the edges of the Solar System. Some comets follow orbits which bring them close into the Solar System and in near proximity to the Sun; others have orbits that take millions of years to complete. Comets are known for their 'tails', these are actually the ice of the comet turning to vapour and being pushed away by solar winds. As a comet travels on its orbit, it loses bits of itself as particles of rock called meteoroids. If one of these should enter into the Earth's atmosphere it forms a meteor or shooting star. Those that occasionally reach the Earth's surface are known as meteorites.

DK Atlas of the Solar System CR-ROM (GSP) is an interactive atlas of the Solar System in 3D, suitable for teaching and learning at Key Stage 2.

Solids
See **states of matter**

Solutions

A solution is a mixture of substances or materials that occurs when a solute (a substance that is dissolved) and solvent (the substance in which dissolving takes place) are mixed during the process of **dissolving**. This takes place at a molecular level. There are many solvents, such as white spirit and other organic solvents. If, however, a substance cannot dissolve in water, it is said to be insoluble.

There are different types of solutions.

- concentrated solutions that contain a large amount of solute;
- dilute solutions that contain only a little solute;
- saturated solutions that cannot hold any more solute.

The process of creating a solution (dissolving) can often be carried out in reverse and the solvent and solute recovered from the solution. This can be done in a number of ways.

- Evaporation occurs when a solution such as salt water is left to dry in the sun. The water evaporates (turns into water vapour) and leaves behind a solid piece of salt.

- Distillation is a process where a solution is heated until it boils. The vapour that is produced is then cooled and the liquid (condensation) collected for use. The distillation process is used in making whisky and gin and in obtaining pure water from seawater.

Sound

Sounds are all around us, some are pleasant, some are unpleasant, yet they are all produced in the same way and that is by something vibrating. Whatever the sound source may be, living or non-living, a vibration takes place for the sound to be produced. The vibrations that are set up by any object cause the molecules of air immediately around the object to also vibrate. This has a knock-on effect as the vibrations alternately push and pull the air molecules together and apart. This pushing together is called compression and the pulling apart decompression or rarefaction. When these compressions and decompressions reach our eardrums they cause the eardrum to vibrate. This vibration is itself transferred to the nervous system where electrical impulses are sent to the brain and the vibrations interpreted and identified as a particular sound. It is not the air that has moved from the sound source to your eardrum, rather it is the repeated compression and decompression of the air particles that go together to make the sound wave.

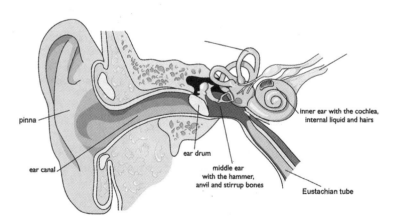

pinna

inner ear with the cochlea, internal liquid and hairs

ear canal

ear drum

middle ear
with the hammer,
anvil and stirrup bones

Eustachian tube

By varying the size and shape of the medium that is vibrating, it is possible to alter the pitch of the sounds produced. Think about musical instruments and you will see that something like a violin, which has short strings and a small sound box, produces high-pitched sound whereas the double bass, a much larger instrument with longer, thicker strings and a larger sound box, produces low-pitched notes. The pitch of the sounds from these instruments can be raised or lowered by changing the length of the strings being vibrated. The pitch of the note is determined by the frequency or the number of waves per second. In order to cause a vibration, energy is used to strike the object in some way; this could be by hitting, plucking or blowing. In the process a transfer of energy takes place, so that sound is actually a type of energy. Using stringed instruments as an example, we can see that when the strings are plucked a vibration is set up. In a small instrument, this vibration occurs quickly and produces a high–pitched sound. In a larger instrument, the vibrations occur more slowly and therefore produce a low–pitched sound. The same can be said for wind instruments, but instead of a material vibrating, like a string, the vibrations this time occur in the column of air in the instrument.

We make a distinction between noise and music although this distinction is influenced by personal references. Generally speaking, noise is a mass of unrelated sound frequencies with no recognisable pattern. Music is usually rhythmic and with many sound frequencies that are mathematically related to each other (doubled, halved, multiples).

As sound travels out from its source, it is able to travel through solids, liquids and gases. Sound actually travels faster and better through solids and liquids than it does through a gas because of the way the molecules are arranged. In solids and liquids, the molecules are more tightly packed than in gases which allows the sound waves to move more easily. The speed of sound in air changes with the temperature of the air. At $0°C$ it travels at 331 m/s whereas at $40°C$ it travels at 354 m/s. However, it is generally accepted that at average temperature, on a clear day, at sea level, sound travels at about 330–340 m/s. This can be compared to 6000 m/s through steel and 1500 m/s through water. (At a speed of about 330 m/s, it travels about 1 000 000 times slower than the speed of light!) Sound waves cannot travel through a vacuum (where there is no air) since in a vacuum there are no particles to vibrate therefore sound will not travel. This explains why space is a silent place. There are no molecules of air in space so when a vibration is made no further waves of vibrations can occur.

When sound waves meet materials, one of three things can occur:

- the sound waves can be reflected creating an echo;
- the sound waves can be transmitted through the material;
- the material can absorb the sound waves.

How a sound wave reacts to a material is dependent upon the individual properties of each material. If the surface is hard and solid and the material is compact such as brick, wood or glass then nearly all of the energy in the sound wave is reflected back. Softer materials with less solid and smooth surfaces reflect much less sound, the material absorbs the rest. Such materials make good soundproofing.

When more **energy** is put into making a vibration, and therefore a sound, there is an increase in the **amplitude** of the sound wave. That is the height of the sound wave is greater and the sound produced is louder. If the frequency of the waves were to be increased then the sound produced would be of a higher pitch. Hence a low-pitched sound has a low frequency and a high-pitched sound a high frequency. There are some sounds that are so high pitched that humans cannot detect them. The range of frequencies that we can detect is called the hearing range and varies depending on the age of people. Young people can detect sounds within a frequency range of about 20 Hz to about 20 000 Hz whereas older people can often not hear sounds over 15 000 Hz. Hertz (Hz) is the unit of frequency used in sound waves; one hertz is a frequency of one wave per second.

Species

A species is a group of organisms that are able to breed with each other to produce fertile offspring. They do not normally breed with members of any other species but similar species are able to interbreed which leads to hybrids between species and the evolution of new species. The animal kingdom contains some 400 000 different species and there are between 10 and 20 million species of animals on the Earth. See **classification**.

Speed, distance and time

The speed of an object relates to us how fast it is moving and is usually measured in metres per second (m/s) or kilometres per hour (km/h). The speed of an object can be calculated by dividing the distance it travels by the time it takes. For example, a car travelling at 60 km in 1 hour would be travelling at a speed of 60 km/h.

$$\text{Speed} = \frac{\text{Distance}}{\text{Time}}$$

Stars

A star is a ball of hot, glowing gases that are reacting with each other in a similar way to the reaction that takes place in a nuclear reactor. It is this reaction, which is called nuclear fusion, which produces the light emitted by a star. Stars cluster together to form galaxies with each galaxy containing many different types of stars. Stars are light sources. The nearest one to **Earth** is the **Sun** and provides the Earth with light and heat energy. Most stars are made up of the two gases hydrogen and helium, together with small amounts of other elements. These gases become compressed at the centre of the star where it becomes so hot and dense that nuclear fusion occurs. This process results in the star releasing energy from its core to the surface from where it is released as light and heat. As stars reach this point, they are said to have joined the Main Sequence and are classified according to their mass.

- High mass stars are the largest, hottest and brightest Main Sequence stars and are blue, blue/white or white in colour. They have masses between three and sixty times greater than that of the Sun and use their hydrogen fuel very quickly so are short-lived. Their temperatures range from about 10 000°C to 20 000°C.

- Low mass stars are the smallest, coolest and dimmest Main Sequence stars and are orange, red or brown in colour. They have masses between half and one twelfth that of the Sun and use their hydrogen fuel very slowly, so having much longer lives. Their temperatures range from about 3000°C to about 4700°C.

- Intermediate mass stars have life cycles between the low and high mass stars. They are yellow in colour and the **Sun** is a good example of an intermediate mass star. They have temperatures of about 6000°C.

Stars are often viewed as part of a constellation or group of stars. Many years ago, astronomers divided stars into groups and, to help them remember them, they drew imaginary pictures around the group (e.g. the Great Bear). This was the start of the system of constellations that we have today. In fact, the stars are largely unrelated and only appear to make these groups when seen from Earth. In reality, they may be many light years away from each other and in another plane (they are not all on the same flat plane as we see them).

Astronomers have also classified stars according to their brightness or magnitude. This is only an apparent magnitude as seen from Earth and does not describe the stars' real brightness. The scale is numerical with 1 being the brightest. Stars classified 1 to 6 are those visible with the naked eye from the Earth, of which there are about 6000.

States of matter

States of matter describe how materials can be solids, liquids or gases. Since everything is made up from tiny particles called **atoms** and **molecules**, it is the arrangement of such particles that determines whether a material is a solid, a liquid or a gas.

- *Solids.* In a solid material, the particles that make up the materials are packed tightly together in a regular pattern and have a very small space between them. They vibrate at a low energy level and each particle is bonded strongly to its neighbouring particles. Solid materials are not easily compressed and retain a fixed shape (unless subjected to a force), have a fixed volume and can be either heavy or light.

- *Liquids.* In a liquid, the particles are much less tightly packed, are not arranged in a regular pattern and are free to slide over one another. They have fairly weak bonds with neighbouring particles. Liquids are not easily compressed, have no fixed shape, have a fixed volume and can also be heavy or light. Liquid particles have more energy than solids.

- *Gas.* In a gas, the particles are widely spread and are not arranged in any regular pattern. They are free to move around in any direction and are not bonded to any neighbouring particles. Gases can be compressed, have no fixed shape, a variable volume and are very light. Gas particles have the most energy of all states of matter.

Solid particles vibrate in fixed positions		An analogy would be a packed supermarket display of oranges
Liquid particles vibrate but can change positions		Liquids will diffuse into each other slowly (e.g. milk in coffee)
Gas particles move around freely at high speed		Particles of gas from coffee going into air and spreading

	Volume	Shape	Density	Particle movement
Solid	Definite	Definite	High	Slow
Liquid	Definite	Takes shape of the bottom of the container	Medium	Medium
Gas	Fills container	Takes the shape of the whole container	Low	Fast

If you placed a solid material on a table, it would retain its shape and stay on the table. A liquid would not retain its shape but would spread out on the tabletop. A gas would have no shape and would not remain on the table; instead its particles would float around freely in the room.

If the temperature of a material is changed, then its state can also be subject to change. If a solid is heated, then it will change into a liquid. If the temperature were raised still further, it would become a gas. Water is a good example. Between certain temperatures (0°C and 100°C) water remains as a liquid, but if the temperature is lowered to below 0°C (freezing point for water) then it will become a solid in the form of ice. In reality, water begins to freeze at 4°C and below. Water is at its most dense at this temperature. Ice has a lower density than water and this is why it floats. This is particularly important for life in rivers and ponds. The water stays liquid beneath the ice, partly insulated by the ice, and is a unique way of ensuring the survival of living things below the ice. Raising the temperature to above 100°C (boiling point) causes the liquid to change into steam, which is a gas. Changes like these take place in other materials and substances with the changes between the states of matter taking place at different temperatures.

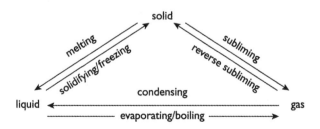

Static electricity

The **electricity** in an electric **current** is a flow of negatively charged electrons along a conductive material. Static electricity is an electrical charge that does not move. When different materials are rubbed together, there is a build up of static electricity caused by **friction**. The crackles associated with static electricity are cause by the electricity discharging from a material. Friction causes the electrons from the atoms that make up the material to be rubbed of onto the other material meaning that it now has more electrons than protons and so is positively charged. Static electricity can be experienced when you rub a balloon on a woollen jumper or when you take a pullover off and hear the crackles of static electricity being discharged.

Lightning is another example of static electricity. The movement of ice particles in a cloud causes the top of the cloud to become positively charged and the bottom negatively charged. As the two attempt to balance themselves out, electricity is discharged and a flash can be seen in the cloud. If the charges within the cloud are strong enough, they force a pathway to the ground to discharge the static electricity.

Stretch and compression

Springs of varying sizes have an equally varying range of uses, from the tiny spring in a ballpoint pen to the suspension springs on large vehicles, but all work in the same way. When a mass is hung from a spring, the **force** of **gravity** pulling on the mass pulls the spring and causes it to stretch. The spring itself can support this weight because it in turn exerts a force on the mass. While the pull in the spring is called 'tension', the opposite of stretching, in this sense, is compression. When a spring is compressed, a force is exerted by the spring on whatever is causing the compression, at the same time as the mass compressing the spring is also exerting a force. For example, if you were to sit on a sprung chair your mass, together with gravity, would exert a downward force upon the springs causing them to compress. At the same time the springs are exerting an upward force on you. When the two forces are equal, you will stop sinking into the chair and remain still. The upward force from the springs is effectively supporting you. Springs, then, can exert two forces: a stretching force and a compression force.

Elastic bands are slightly different. Springs stretch and compress because of the way the material has been shaped; the actual material the spring is made from only stretches to a limited extent. However, some materials do stretch rather more and still return to their original size when the force on them is removed. These materials are said to be elastic. Whilst the spring may be said to have elastic properties, its material does not stretch as those that are elastic. This is not compression since the material is merely returning to its original shape. When elastic materials are extended too far, they reach a 'yield point' and no longer retain their elasticity.

Substances

There are very many materials all around us. Some occur naturally, while others are manufactured. These materials, such as air, water, sand, paper, wood and steel are each different and distinctive and are called substances (although the terms materials and substances are often seen as synonymous). Those that are naturally occurring are the raw materials from which we make other useful substances. The process of manufacture invariably involves a kind of **chemical change or reaction**.

Source of raw materials	Substances manufactured
Air	Oxygen, nitrogen, argon
Coal	Coke, plastics, detergents, perfumes
Oil	Petrol, diesel, lubricants, plastics
Plants	Foods, timber, dyes, rubber, cotton
Rocks	Sand, bricks, glass, metals
Sea	Salt, magnesium

Sun

The Sun is the nearest star to the **Earth** and is the centre of our **Solar System**. Like all **stars**, it is a ball of hot gas within which nuclear fusion takes place. The Sun, which was born some 5000 million years ago, has a temperature at its centre of around 14 000 000°C, whereas the surface is a cooler 6,000°C. It is no longer the only star known to have a system of planets around it (astronomers are discovering others all the time) and is the provider of energy for life here on Earth. Indeed, all energy sources can be traced back to the Sun and, without it, life here on Earth would quite simply not exist.

The Sun is not only extremely hot, it is immense in size. It has a mass of approximately 1.99×10^{30} kg and a diameter of 1 392 000 km and is 149 000 000 km away from the Earth. Even so the light that the Sun provides, travelling at a speed of 300 000 km/sec, takes 8.3 minutes to arrive here on Earth. The Sun like all bodies in the Solar System, is rotating about an axis. However, unlike the planets, and because its surface consists of layers of gas, different parts of the Sun rotate at different speeds. The middle part, around its equator, takes around 25 days to rotate once, whereas the top and bottom, around the poles take about 30 days. The layers of gas that make up the Sun are:

- the photosphere which is about 300 km to 400 km thick with gas swirls and bubbles that give the Sun a mottled appearance. It is the photosphere that can be seen as the Sun rises and sets;

- the chromopshere which is some 2000 km thick and can only be seen during a **solar eclipse**;

- the corona which is the outer layer and is millions of kilometres thick. The corona can only be seen during solar eclipses.

Suspension

A suspension is formed when very small insoluble solids are mixed with a liquid (e.g. flour mixed with water).

Teeth

The hardest part of the human body is the surface of the teeth. Made from enamel, this surface protects the teeth from being worn away and attacked by chemicals. Teeth play a vital role in the initial stages of food digestion in that, before it is swallowed, food is chewed. Most mammals have specialised teeth that are shaped in particular ways to carry out different tasks. Teeth are used to bite food, break it up and grind it into small pieces. Humans are omnivores – we eat both plants and animals as food, and our teeth are capable of eating both, unlike some other animals. Carnivores or meat eaters have teeth suited to killing other animals and tearing their flesh, whereas herbivores, plant eaters, have teeth more suited to eating grass. As humans we have different types of teeth, each of which has a different function.

Tooth type	Shape	Function
Incisors	Sharp, chisel shape	Biting off food, cutting food
Canines	Sharp, pointed shape	Biting off food, tearing food
Molars/premolars	Flat and blunt shape	Grinding, chewing and crushing food

- Canine teeth are located one on either side of the front teeth or incisors. They are more pointed than the incisors and molars as they are used for gripping and tearing food.

- Incisors are the teeth located at the front of the mouth. They are chisel shaped and used for cutting food.

- Molars are the set of teeth located at the sides/back of the mouth. They are large, flat teeth and this shape together with their bumpy surface makes them ideal for grinding and crushing food.

Human babies are generally born without teeth and by the age of one their milk teeth have appeared. Between the ages of 6 and 12, these milk teeth are replaced by permanent teeth. The table below shows how many of each tooth we usually have:

Age	Tooth set	Tooth type/No.	Total number
Birth	None		None
1 year	Milk teeth	Incisors 8 Canine 4 Premolars 8	20
6–12 Adults	Permanent	Incisors 8 Canine 4 Premolars 4 Molars 12	32

We lose our milk teeth as we grow. We can and do lose our permanent teeth for a variety of reasons: through injury, gum disease or tooth decay. It is important though that we maintain healthy teeth for as long as possible so that we can chew properly and also be spared the pain of a decaying tooth. Most adults have 32 teeth in their second or permanent set consisting of:

- 8 incisors
- 4 canines
- 8 premolars
- 12 molars

The part of the tooth you can see is the crown, which is about half of the full tooth. The crown is covered with enamel, below which is a layer of dentine. The centre of the tooth is filled with a soft pulp which contains the blood supply and nerve endings. Long roots anchor the tooth into the jaw.

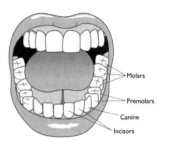
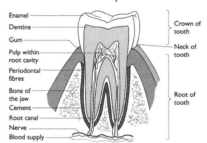

The British Dental Health Foundation (http://www.dentalhealth.org.uk/ funbit/index.htm) have a number of resources to download for use with Key Stages 1 and 2 children during a dental health topic.

Temperature

Temperature is a measure of how hot something is. It is a measure of the kinetic energy of the particles in an object, which is the speed at which they are travelling. If the particles are travelling quickly, then the temperature of the body will be higher; as the particles slow down so too the temperature is lowered. Temperature is different from **heat** in that heat is a form of energy and as this energy is transferred to another body it causes the temperature to rise.

There are three temperature scales:

Scale	Named after	Details
Celsius	Anders Celsius (1701–1744)	Freezing point: 0°C Boiling point: 100°C
Fahrenheit	Daniel Fahrenheit (1686–1736)	Freezing point: 32°F Boiling point: 212°F
Kelvin	Lord Kelvin (1824–1907)	Starts at the lowest possible temperature, called absolute zero, approx. −273°C

Tides

The movement of the Earth's seas and oceans can be seen twice daily when the tide comes in and goes out. The cause of this movement is a complex relationship between forces.

- Seas and oceans on the side of the Earth that are nearest the Moon are pulled upwards by the Moon's gravitational effect. This is also repeated on the opposite side of the Earth, causing two bulges and troughs in the oceans.

- As the Earth spins, the bulges in the oceans created by these gravitational forces stay more or less in the same place while the Earth spins underneath them. The result is that most shorelines have two high tides and two low tides as the landmasses pass the troughs and waves.

At full and new moons, the tidal force of the Sun (usually a lesser effect) is added to that of the Moon causing high spring tides, while at quarter moons the forces are opposed causing low neap tides.

Transpiration and translocation

The movement of water through a plant is called transpiration. It happens because plants need water to survive. The water travels from the roots and stem to the leaves where it evaporates into the atmosphere though the stomata.

Translocation, on the other hand, often works in the other direction. It carries food substances away from the leaves into the buds, shoots and roots of the plant.

Universe

The Universe is described as being everything you can possibly imagine including space. It is simply all existing things, from the smallest possible object, living or non-living, to the largest mass in space. Scientists think that the Universe was born in a huge explosion, called the Big Bang, about 13 000–15 000 million years ago. In that explosion, all matter, energy, space and time were created and the process of the expansion of the Universe, which continues today, began. Minutes after the Big Bang, helium and hydrogen were formed which over millions of years came together, due to gravity, to produce galaxies of stars.

Years after the Big Bang	Event
About 1000 million	Hydrogen and helium come together.
About 3000 million	Galaxies start to take shape.
About 5000 million	Our galaxy – the Milky Way – is formed.
About 8000 million	The Sun is 'born'.
About 10 000 million	The first life forms appeared on Earth.

Variation

Within the many millions of species of living organisms in the world, there are many individual differences. These variations occur because, while the members of a species may all look alike, each has its own unique **DNA** and is therefore a unique mix of genetic coding from its parents. This means that while individual specimens within a species will each have a set of distinct characteristics, there will be sufficient similarities to be able to identify them as belonging to a particular species.

Sometimes, within a family group, these differences are quite marked, with brothers and sisters, for example, sharing the same parents but having different characteristics. These variations are important since they mean the species will change and develop or evolve over a period of time. These changes and variations may be responses to environmental factors as a species is forced to adapt in order to survive and thrive in varying environmental conditions (e.g. urban foxes). These factors can include the availability of food, climate change, danger of predators and in some cases, the effects of man's presence.

Nevertheless, all permanent changes in variation are the results of mutations. Mutations are spontaneous errors that occur during the replication of DNA. As the cells are copied and divide, errors can and do occur or damage is caused to the DNA. Often this damage can be automatically repaired. If not repaired, the DNA coding is permanently changed and a new piece of genetic code is created. This is called a **mutation** and creates a new characteristic within the individuals in the species. Some mutations have little effect; others are more noticeable. Mutations that occur in the sex cells of animals can be passed on from one generation to the next.

The world we live in is the result of mutations that have been effective in ensuring the survival of a species. The light-sensitive cells in our eyes are the result of mutations in animals millions of years ago. However, some mutations are less beneficial, such as sickle cell anaemia or thalassaemia in humans. Even these mutations must have been beneficial under some conditions (e.g. sickle cells are reported to give added immunity from malaria).

Some variations within a species occur due to environmental factors and are not part of DNA and therefore are not passed on. For example, if a particular plant or animal is able to live and grow in an area that has a plentiful food source, it will thrive and be healthy. Humans who are extremely athletic or fit and live very healthy lives will not necessarily produce offspring with these characteristics. However, since these characteristics are a result of environmental factors and not inherited genetically, there is the possibility that the offspring will have opportunities and be brought up in an environment where particular characteristics are encouraged.

Velocity

Velocity is used to describe not only speed but also the direction of travel. Whereas speed describes how fast something is moving, velocity specifies the direction. A car with a speed of 60 km/h, travelling east, would have a velocity of 60 km/h in an easterly direction.

Vertebrates

Vertebrates are animals, such as fish, amphibians, reptiles, birds and mammals, which have a backbone and a **skeletal system** inside their bodies. Together they form the largest number of species within the phylum of chordates. A phylum is a major grouping in the animal kingdom. In most cases, this skeletal system is made from bone although there are some species of fish whose skeletons are made of cartilage.

Voltage

In an electrical circuit, a cell or battery may be used to provide the electrons with electrical potential energy. They then move around the circuit from the negative to the positive terminals. As they leave the negative terminal, the electrons have a high electrical potential energy. When they meet a component, such as a lamp, some of that energy is transferred out as heat or light. The electrons return to the positive terminal with less energy. There is therefore a difference between the levels at negative and positive terminals. This difference is measured by the potential difference or voltage. The greater the voltage of a cell or battery, the more energy it is able to provide.

Water

About two-thirds of the Earth's surface is covered by water, the human body is around 65% water and a tomato contains 95% water. These simple facts illustrate how important water is to life on earth. For life to continue living things require water.

Water cycle

The water cycle is an important part of life here on Earth and is the natural method of moving water around the planet so that the plants and animals living on the Earth can benefit from it. The water cycle involves a number of processes.

- *Evaporation.* Water from the surface of the Earth, in the oceans, seas and rivers, is heated by the Sun causing **evaporation** to take place. This then rises up with warm air. The air rises either because it has been warmed by the Earth and the Sun or because cooler air has come under it lifting it higher.

- *Transpiration.* As part of its internal transport system of moving water and nutrients about, a plant can lose large amounts of water by evaporation through its leaves. This process is called transpiration and in large trees can see 1000 litres of water being lost to the atmosphere.

- *Condensation.* As the evaporated water rises with rising air, in the form of water vapour, it meets cooler air and begins to cool down and condenses. This condensed water vapour now takes on the form of water droplets, which then form clouds.

- *Precipitation.* This is the name we give to water falling to the ground, whether it is as rain, sleet or snow. Most rain, except for that in the tropical areas of the world, actually starts as ice crystals. High in the clouds, the temperature is so low that ice crystals form and as more water vapour freezes onto these crystals, they increase in size. These crystals remain in the cloud as long as the rising air inside the cloud is able to cause an upthrust great enough to overcome the effects of gravity. As the crystals continue to grow, this becomes impossible and so they begin to fall as snow. If the air is cold enough, they will continue to fall as snowflakes; if the air is warmer, the snowflakes will melt and become water, falling as rain.

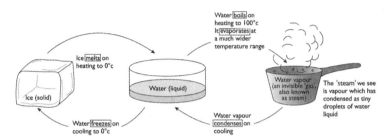

Water boils on heating to 100°c It evaporates at a much wider temperature range

Ice melts on heating to 0°c

Ice (solid)

Water (liquid)

Water freezes on cooling to 0°c

Water vapour condenses on cooling

Water vapour (an invisible 'gas', also known as steam)

The 'steam' we see is vapour which has condensed as tiny droplets of water liquid

INTERFACT Water CD-ROM (Two-Can Publishing) is a 48-page information-tion book and interactive CD-Rom with games, quizzes and puzzles appropriate for use with children in Key Stage 2.

Watts

The rate of use of energy or the power of a system is measured in watts. When electricity flows through a component in a circuit, the power is equal to the voltage multiplied by the current. So, a 240-volt appliance using a current of 5 amps will have a power of 1200 watts. If the appliance were to be left running for one hour, it would have used 1200 watt-hours or 1.2-kilowatt hours (kWh) of electricity. This is the measure that is often used to describe the power usage of domestic electrical appliances such as heaters.

Weather

The weather is something that affects many living things and influences many aspects of their behaviour and growth. The weather is described as being the state of the air in a particular place at any one time. It can be hot or cold, dry or wet, windy or calm, can change very quickly and is a description of short-term change. Long-term changes and patterns, however, describe the **climate** of a region.

- *Air pressure*. The gravitational pull exerted on the atmosphere is air pressure. We do not normally feel it because the pressure inside our bodies is the same as it is outside. At ground level, the air pressure is greatest because there is more air overhead. Then, as you travel upwards, the air pressure is reduced because there is less air. The level of air pressure can affect the weather: when there is high pressure the air mass is descending, cold air sinks to the ground and as it becomes stable it gets warmer, absorbs moisture and usually brings fine weather. Low pressure occurs when warm air rises, reducing the air pressure nearer the surface of the Earth. This warm air then condenses into clouds so that low pressure can bring rain.

- **Clouds**. Clouds form when evaporated water, now water vapour, condenses (see **water cycle**). Clouds are an indication of the weather to come and can be seen in one of three basic types:

Cloud type	Characteristics and weather
Cirrus	Cirrus clouds form high in the sky and are an indication that fine weather may be ending and rain is possible.
Cumulus	Cumulus clouds are puffy white clouds with a flat base. Because they are formed from rising bubbles of warm air (thermals) they are often seen when the weather is generally warm and fine.
Stratus	Stratus clouds form in layers that can reach across large areas of sky. The weather they bring is rain or light snow.

- **Temperature**. This varies both globally around the **Earth** and more locally in particular regions. There is also variation between different times of the day and between the **seasons**.

- **Winds**. The air is always moving around the Earth and as it does so the weather changes. Winds occur because of the differences in air pressure and temperature around the world, with movement from high-pressure areas to low-pressure areas. The rotation of the Earth is another factor in the movement of air and winds.

The weather conditions experienced on Earth include:

- **Rainfall**. See **water cycle**.

- **Thunder and lightning**. Inside a storm cloud water and ice particles collide creating a build up of **static electricity**. Positive charges are at the top of the cloud and negative charges at the bottom, trying to escape to the ground. When the difference between the two charges is large enough, a lightning stroke flashes either from the top to the bottom of the cloud or from the bottom to the ground. The lightning heats the air around it to temperatures of about 25 000°C to 30 000°C. This causes the air to expand rapidly, even faster than the speed of sound and creates the crash of thunder. We see the lightning first since **light** travels faster than **sound**.

- **Sunshine**. All weather conditions happen because **heat** from the **Sun** keeps the air on the move. As the surface of the **Earth** heats up, so too does the air. The hot air rises, cooler air replaces it causing winds to occur. Heat from the Sun also makes water evaporate from the seas and form clouds.

- *Hail, snow and sleet.* Hailstones develop inside tall cumulo-nimbus clouds. Strong currents within the cloud can lift raindrops high into the frozen top part of the cloud. The raindrop then freezes and falls back down the cloud. When it is tossed back up the cloud, another layer of ice is added. This continues until the hailstone falls to the ground. Snow is formed when ice crystals in clouds join together. When they fall from the cloud they will reach the ground as snow if the temperature of the air is freezing all the way down. If it is too warm, the crystals may evaporate back into water vapour or melt and fall as sleet or rain. While sleet is usually half melted snow, it can also be half frozen rain that forms when raindrops evaporate and cool as they fall.

- *Fog and mist.* Fog and mist are clouds that have formed near the ground. Like all clouds, they are made when the air is full of water vapour. If the visibility in this cloud is between one and two kilometres it is called mist; if the visibility is less than one kilometre the cloud is called fog.

The Met Office (http://www.meto.gov.uk/education/curriculum/index.html) offer online resources for teaching and learning at Key Stages 1 and 2, including worksheets and classroom activities.

Years and light years

A year is the time taken for the Earth to orbit the Sun once. More precisely, it is 365.25 days. The ¼ days are added together every four years to give a leap year of 366 days. The spin of the Earth is in fact slowing down. Scientists have determined, from growth lines on coral, that the length of a year some 400 million years ago was about 400 days because the Earth was spinning faster and so the days were shorter. The slowing down of the rotation of the Earth is a very gradual process and is due in part to the friction of the tides as they drag water backwards and forwards around the Earth.

A light year, on the other hand, is in fact not a measure of time but of distance. It is the distance light travels in a calendar year and can be calculated as 365 (number of days in a year) × 24 (hours in a day) x 60 (minutes in an hour) × 60 (seconds in a minute) × 300 000 (the speed of light). This means that the distance travelled by light in one year is 94.6 billion kilometres. After the Sun, our nearest star is 4.6 light years away or 397.32 billion kilometres and light from there takes 4.6 years to reach the Earth. Light from even more distant stars and galaxies takes hundreds and even millions of years to reach us. With such huge distances involved, it is possible that some of the stars we think we see now no longer exist. We will not know until the light from them ceases to arrive here.

The table below references the **DfEE/QCA** Schemes of Work with the National Curriculum requirements. It gives indicative references to appropriate sections in this book. The references to information in each section is not age-specific, so, for example, children studying Unit 1A are not expected to know all the detail in the listed sections. These entries are designed to help the teacher to have a deeper understanding and knowledge.

QCA Schemes of Work unit	NC reference	Key concepts covered in this book
1A Ourselves	**Sc2** 1a, 1b, 2a, 2g, 4a	Human body, Living things, Nervous system, Senses and sensitivity
1B Growing plants	**Sc 2** 1b, 2a, 2b, 2c, 2e, 3a, 3b, 5b, 5c	Healthy plants, Plants
1C Sorting and using materials	**Sc3** 1a, 1b, 1c, 1d	Magnetism, Materials
1D Light and dark	**Sc2** 2g **Sc4** 3a, 3b	Light, Reflection, Sun
1E Pushes and pulls	**Sc4** 2a, 2b, 2c	Forces, Movement
1F Sound and hearing	**Sc2** 2g, **Sc4** 3c, 3d	Sound
2A Health and growth	**Sc2** 2b, 2f, 2g	Growth, Healthy humans, Nutrition, Reproduction
2B Plants and animals in the local environment	**Sc2** 2f, 3c, 5b, 5c	Animals, Ecosystems, Environment, Habitats, Healthy plants, Plants, Reproduction
2C Variation	**Sc2** 1a, 2e, 4a, 4b, 5b	Adaptation, Classification, Species, Variation
2D Grouping and changing materials	**Sc3** 1c, 1d, 2a, 2b	Burning, Elasticity, Magnetism, Materials, Melting, States of matter
2E Forces and movement	**Sc3** 2a **Sc4** 2a, 2b, 2c	Forces, Movement
2F Using electricity	**Sc4** 1a, 1b, 1c	Batteries, Circuits, Current, Electrical components, Electricity,
3A Teeth and eating	**Sc2** 1a, 1b, 1c	Balanced Diets, Healthy humans, Nutrition, Teeth
3B Helping plants grow well	**Sc2** 1b, 2b, 3a, 3b, 3c	Growth, Healthy plants, Nutrition, Plants, Photosynthesis, Pollination
3C Characteristics of materials	**Sc3** 1a	Materials
3D Rocks and soils	**Sc3** 1a, 1d, 3a	Rocks, Soil
3E Magnets and springs	**Sc4** 2a, 2b, 2e	Electromagnetism, Forces, Magnetism
3F Light and shadows	**Sc4** 3a, 3b, 4b	Colour, Eclipses, Light, Shadows

4A Moving and growing	Sc2 1a, 2c, 2e	Healthy humans, Human body, Movement, Muscular system, Skeletal system
4B Habitats	Sc2 1c, 4a, 4b, 5a, 5b, 5c, 5d, 5e	Animals, Climate, Ecosystems, Environments, Habitats, Plants,
4C Keeping warm	Sc3 1a, 1b, 1c, 2c	Conductors – thermal, Heat, Insulators, Temperature, Thermal energy
4D Solids, liquids and how they can be separated	Sc3 1a, 2a, 2d, 2f, 3a, 3b, 3c, 3e	Chemical changes and reactions, Compounds, Dissolving, Mixtures, Physical changes and reactions, States of matter
4E Friction	Sc4 2c, 2e	Energy, Forces, Friction, Heat, Newtons
4F Circuits and conductors	Sc3 1c Sc4 1a, 1b	Circuits, Batteries, Conductors – electrical, Electricity
5A Keeping healthy	Sc2 1a, 2b, 2c, 2d, 2e, 2g, 2h	Balanced diets, Body systems, Healthy humans
5B Life cycles	Sc2 1a 1b, 2f, 3a, 3d	Animals, Life cycles, Life processes, Plants, Pollination, Reproduction
5C Gases around us	Sc3 1a, 1e, 2b Sc4 2c	Atmosphere, Evaporation, Materials, States of matter
5D Changing state	Sc3 1e, 2c, 2d, 2e	Atoms, Boiling point, Chemical changes and reactions, Condensation, Evaporation, States of matter, Water cycle
5E Earth, Sun and Moon	Sc4 4a, 4b, 4c, 4d	Day and night, Earth, Eclipses, Moon, Solar System, Years and light years
5F Changing sounds	Sc4 3e, 3f, 3g	Energy, Sound
6A Interdependence and adaptation	Sc2 1b, 1c, 3a, 3b, 3c, 4a, 5b, 5c, 5d, 5e	Adaptation, Food chains and webs, Habitats, Nutrition, Plants, Photosynthesis
6B Micro-organisms	Sc2 2b, 2f, 5f	Decay and decomposition, Healthy humans, Micro-organisms, Organisms
6C More about dissolving	Sc3 3a, 3b, 3c, 3d	Dissolving, Evaporation, Separating materials
6D Reversible and irreversible changes	Sc3 2a, 2b, 2f, 2g, 3c, 3d	Burning, Chemical changes and reactions, Compounds, Dissolving, Heat, Mixtures, Physical changes and reactions, States of matter
6E Balanced and unbalanced forces	Sc4 2b, 2c, 2d, 2e	Balanced and unbalanced forces, Forces
6F How we see things	Sc4 3a, 3c, 3d	Light, Reflection, Refraction, Shadows, Sun
6G Changing circuits	Sc4 1a, 1b, 1c	Circuits, Circuit diagrams, Electricity, Electrical components, Conductors – electrical, Insulators

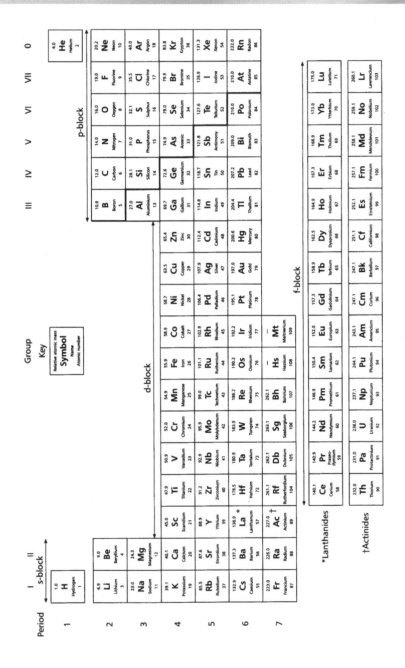

Useful resources

(2001) *100 Science Lessons (Reception to Year 6)*. Leamington Spa: Scholastic.

British Nutrition Foundation Posters. London: British Nutrition Foundation (www.nutrition.org.uk).

Burton, N. (2000) *Pocket Guides to the Primary Curriculum: Physical Processes*. Leamington Spa: Scholastic.

Burton, N. (2001) *Pocket Guides to the Primary Curriculum: Life Processes and Living Things*. Leamington Spa: Scholastic.

Burton, N. (2001) *Pocket Guides to the Primary Curriculum: Materials and Their Properties*. Leamington Spa: Scholastic.

Devereux, J. (2000) *Developing Primary Subject Knowledge in Science*. London: Paul Chapman Publishing.

Farrow, S. (1996) *The Really Useful Science Book*. London: Falmer Press.

Johnsey, R., et al (2002) *Primary Science: Knowledge and Understanding (second edition)*. Exeter: Learning Matters.

Wenham, M. (1995) *Understanding Primary Science Ideas*. London: Paul Chapman Publishing.

Atlas of the Solar System CD-ROM. Dorling Kindersley Multimedia.

Bodywise CD-ROM. Sherston Software (www.sherston.co.uk).

Butterflies, Bugs and Other Beasties CD-ROM. Spiny Software (www.spinysoft.co.uk).

Drug Sense CD-ROM. New Media (www.new-media.co.uk).

Interfact Water CD-ROM. Two-Can Publishing (www.two-canpublishing.com).

Science Fair CD-ROM. Sherston Software (www.sherston.co.uk).

Association for Science in Education – www.ase.org.uk

British Dental Health Foundation – www.dentalhealth.org.uk

Department for Education and Skills – www.dfes.gov.uk

Espesso Productions – www.espresso.co.uk

Hardy Aggregates – www.hardy-aggregates.co.uk

Met Office – www.meto.gov.uk/education

National Grid for Learning – www.ngfl.gov.uk

New Media – www.new-media.co.uk

Qualifications and Curriculum Authority – www.qca.org.uk

Science Museum – www.sciencemuseum.org.uk

Sherston Software – www.sherston.co.uk

Spiny Software – www.spinysoft.co.uk

Two-Can Pubilshing – www.two-canpublishing.com